THE RESURRECTION OF HENRY BOX BROWN AT PHILADELPHIA.

Henry Brown emerges from his box. The black man is William Still, conductor of Philadelphia's Underground Railroad.

Narrative of the Life of Henry Box Brown

HENRY BOX BROWN.

The following remarkable incident exhibits the cruelty of the slave system, while it shows the ingenuity and desperate determination of its victims to escape from it :—

A few months ago, a slave in a Southern city managed to open a correspondence with a gentleman in a Northern city, with a view to effect his escape from bondage. Having arranged the preliminaries, he paid somebody $40 to box him up, and mark him, "This side up, with care," and take him to the Express office, consigned to his friend at the North. On the passage, being on board of a steamboat, he was accidentally turned head downward, and almost died with the rush of blood to the head. At the next change of transportation, however, he was turned right side up again; and after twenty-six hours' confinement, arrived safely at his destination. On receiving the box, the gentleman had doubts whether he should find a corpse or a living man. He tapped lightly on the box, with the question, "All right?" and was delighted to hear the response, "All right, sir." The poor fellow was immediately liberated from his place of burial.*

An engraving from *The Liberty Almanac*. William Still is not pictured.

Courtesy, American Antiquarian Society.

DOVER · THRIFT · EDITIONS

Narrative of the Life of Henry Box Brown

Henry Box Brown

DOVER PUBLICATIONS, INC.
Mineola, New York

DOVER THRIFT EDITIONS

GENERAL EDITOR: MARY CAROLYN WALDREP
EDITOR OF THIS VOLUME: ALISON DAURIO

Bibliographical Note

This Dover edition, first published in 2015, is an unabridged republication of the work originally published by Oxford University Press in 2002.

Library of Congress Cataloging-in-Publication Data

Narrative of the life of Henry Box / Henry Box Brown. — Dover edition.
    p. cm.
Originally published: Oxford University Press, 2002.
ISBN-13: 978-0-486-79575-1
ISBN-10: 0-486-79575-6
    1. Brown, Henry Box, 1815 or 1816. 2. Fugitive slaves-Virgina—Biography.
3. African americans—virginia—Biography. 4. Slavery—Virgina—History—19th century. 5. African American abolitionists—Biography.

E450.873 2015
326'.8092—dc23

                                                                    2014048468

Manufactured in the United States by Courier Corporation
79575601   2015
www.doverpublications.com

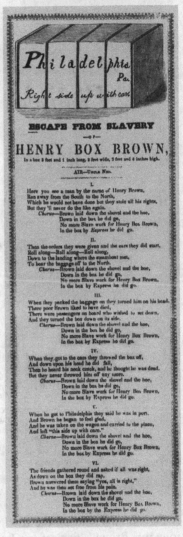

This 1849 broadside contains the full text of Brown's parody of "Uncle Ned." Brown probably sold copies at his lectures.

Courtesy, American Antiquarian Society.

Engraving of the Box in which HENRY BOX BROWN escaped from slavery in Richmond, Va.

SONG,

Sung by Mr. Brown on being removed from the box.

I waited patiently for the Lord ;—
And he, in kindness to me, heard my calling—
And he hath put a new song into my mouth—
Even thanksgiving—even thanksgiving—
    Unto our God!

Blessed—blessed is the man
That has set his hope, his hope in the Lord !
O Lord ! my God ! great, great is the wondrous work
    Which thou hast done !

If I should declare them—and speak of them—
They would be more than I am able to express.
I have not kept back thy love, and kindness, and truth,
    From the great congregation !

Withdraw not thou thy mercies from me,
Let thy love, and kindness, and thy truth, alway preserve me—
Let all those that seek thee be joyful and glad !
    Be joyful and glad !

And let such as love thy salvation—
Say always—say always—
The Lord be praised !
    The Lord be praised !

Laing's Steam Press, 1 1-2 Water Street, Boston.

A Boston engraving of the text of the 40th Psalm. Singing this song was Brown's first act as a free person.

Courtesy, American Antiquarian Society.

This image was used to advertise Brown's book, but it also appeared on the cover of an 1854 book on the famous runaway
Anthony Burns.

Author's collection.

HENRY BOX BROWN.

I will tell you the story of Henry Box Brown. It is a strange tale, and it is all true. Henry was a slave in Richmond, Virginia, and then his name was Henry Brown. He had a wife and four little children whom he loved very much.

One night when he went home to his little hut, his children and their mother, were gone, and poor Henry found they had been sold to a trader, and were taken away to Carolina. It made him almost crazy to hear this dreadful

An illustration from an 1849 book of children's stories.

PREFACE

by Henry Box Brown

So much has already been written concerning the evils of slavery, and by men so much more able to portray its horrid form than I am, that I might well be excused if I were to remain altogether silent on the subject; but however much has been written, however much has been said, and however much has been done, I feel impelled by the voice of my own conscience, from the recent experience which I have had of the alarming extent to which the traffic in human beings is carried on, and the cruelties, both bodily and mental, to which men in the condition of slaves are continually subjected, and also from the hardening and blasting influences which this traffic produces on the character of those who thus treat as goods and chattels the bodies and souls of their fellows, to add yet one other testimony of, and protest against, the foul blot on the state of morals, of religion, and of cultivation in the American republic. For I feel convinced that enough has not been written, enough has not been said, enough has not been done, while nearly four millions of human beings, possessing immortal souls, are, in chains, dragging out their existence in the southern states. They are keenly alive to the heaven born voice of liberty, and require the illumination of the grace of Almighty God. Having, myself, been in that same position, but by the blessing of God having been enabled to snap my chains and escape to a land of liberty—I owe it as a sacred duty to the cause of humanity, that I should devote my life to the redemption of my fellow men.

The tale of my own sufferings is not one of great interest to those who delight to read of hair-breadth adventures, of tragic occurrences, and scenes of blood—my life, even in slavery, has been in many respects comparatively comfortable. I have experienced a continuance of such kindness, as slaveholders have to bestow; but though my body has escaped the lash of the whip, my mind has groaned under tortures which I believe will never be related, because, language is inadequate to express them, but those know them who have them to endure. The whip, the cowskin, the gallows, the stocks, the paddle, the prison, the perversion of the stomach—although bloody and barbarous in their nature—have no comparison with those internal pangs which are felt by the soul when the hand of the merciless tyrant plucks from one's bosom the object of one's ripened affections, and the darlings who in requiring parental care, confer the sweet sensations of parental bliss. I freely admit I have enjoyed my full share of all those blessings which fall to the lot of a slave's existence. I have felt the sweet influence of friendships' power, and the still more delightful glow of love; and had I never heard the name of liberty or seen the tyrant lift his cruel hand to smite my fellow and my friend, I might perhaps have dragged my chains in quietude to the grave, and have found a tomb in a slavery-polluted land; but thanks be to God I heard the glorious sound and felt its inspiring influence on my heart, and having satisfied myself of the value of freedom. I resolved to purchase it whatever should be its price.

INTRODUCTION

by Henry Box Brown

While America is boasting of her freedom and making the world ring with her professions of equality, she holds millions of her inhabitants in bondage. This surely must be a wonder to all who seriously reflect on the subject of man holding property in man, in a land of republican institutions. That slavery, in all its phases, is demoralizing to every one concerned, none who may read the following narrative, can for a moment doubt. In my opinion unless the Americans purge themselves of this stain, they will have to undergo very severe, if not protracted suffering. It is not at all unlikely that the great unsettledness which of late has attached to the prices of cotton; the very unsatisfactory circumstance of that slaveholding continent being the principal field employed in the production of that vegetable, by the dealing in, and the manufacture of, which, such astonishing fortunes have been amassed—will lead to arrangements being entered into, through the operation of which the bondmen will be made free. The popular mind is, in every land becoming impatient of its chains; and soon the American captives will be made to taste of that freedom, which by right, belongs to man. The manner in which this mighty change will be accomplished, may *not* be at present understood, but with the Lord all things are possible. It may be, that the very means which are being used by those who wish to perpetuate slavery, and to recapture those who have by any plans not approved of by those dealers in human flesh, become free, will be amongst the instruments which God will employ to overturn the whole system.

Another means which, in addition to the above, we think, will contribute to the accomplishment of this desirable object—the destruction of slavery—is the simple, but natural narrations of those who have been long under the yoke themselves. It is a lamentable fact that some ministers of religion are contaminated with the foulness of slavery. Those men, in the southern states, who ascend the pulpit to proclaim the world's jubilee, are themselves, in fearful numbers, the holders of slaves! When we reflect on the bar which slavery constituted to the advancement of the objects at one time contemplated by the almost defunct "Evangelical Alliance"; when we consider that Great Being who beheld the Israelites in their captivity, and beholding, came down to deliver them is still the same; have we not reason to believe that he will in his Providence raise up another Moses, to guide the now enslaved sons of Ham to the privileges which humanity, irrespective of colour or clime, is always at liberty to demand. While the British mind retains its antipathy to slavery in all its kinds, and sends forth its waves of audibly expressed opinion on the subject, that opinion, meeting with one nearly allied in character to itself in the Northern States; and while both unite in tending towards the South the reiterated demand for an honest acting, one those turgid profession of equality peculiar to all American proceedings—in every thing but slavery—the Southern states must yield to the pressure from without; even the slaves will feel themselves growing beyond the dimensions which their chains can enclose, and backed by the roar of the British Lion, and supported by Northern Americans in their just demand for emancipation, the long downtrodden and despised bondmen will arise, and by a united voice assert their title to freedom. It may be that the subject of the following narrative has a mission from God to the human family. Certainly the deliverance of Moses, from destruction on the Nile, was scarcely more marvellous than was the deliverance of Mr. Henry Box Brown from the horrors of slavery. For any lengthy observations, by which the reader will be detained from the subject of the following pages, there can be no necessity whatever.

Mr. Brown was conveyed from Richmond, Virginia, to Philadelphia in a box, three feet long, and two feet six inches deep. For twenty-seven hours he was enclosed in this box. The following copy of a letter which was written by the gentleman to whom it was directed, will explain this part of the subject:—

Copy of a Letter respecting Henry Box Brown's escape from Slavery— a verification of Patrick Henry's Speech in Virginia

Legislature, March, 1775, when he said, *"Give me Liberty or give me Death."*

Philadelphia, March 26th, 1849.

DEAR——

Here is a man who has been the hero of one of the most extraordinary achievements I ever heard of;—he came to me on Saturday Morning last, in a box tightly hooped, marked "THIS SIDE UP," by *overland express, from the city of Richmond!!* Did you ever hear of any thing in all your life to beat that? Nothing that was done on the barricades of Paris exceeded this cool and deliberate intrepidity. To appreciate fully the boldness and risk of the achievement, you ought to see the box and hear all the circumstances. The box is in the clear three feet one inch long, two feet six inches deep, and two feet wide. It was a regular old store box, such as you see in Pearl street;—it was grooved at the joints and braced at the ends, leaving but the very slightest crevice to admit the air. Nothing saved him from suffocation but the free use of the water—a quantity of which he took in with him in a beef's bladder, and with which he bathed his face — and the constant fanning of himself with his hat. He fanned himself unremittingly all the time. The "this side up" on the box was not regarded, and he was twice put with his head downward, resting with his back against the end of the box, his feet braced against the other,—the first time he succeeded in shifting his position; but the second time was on board of the steam boat, where people were sitting and standing about the box, and where any motions inside would have been overheard and have led to discovery; he was therefore obliged to keep his position *for twenty miles.* This nearly killed him. He says the veins in his temples were as thick as his finger. I had been expecting him for several days, and was in mortal fear all the time lest his arrival should only be a signal for calling in the coroner. You can better imagine than I can describe my sensations, when, in answer to my rap on the box and question, *"all right,"* the prompt response came "all right, sir." The man weighs 200 pounds, and is about five feet eight inches in height; and is, as you will see, a noble looking fellow. He will tell you the whole story. Please send him on to Mr. McGleveland, Boston, with this letter, to save me the time it would take to write another. He was boxed up in Richmond, at five, A.M. on Friday shipped at eight, and I opened him up at six (about daylight) next morning. He has a sister in New Bedford.

Yours, truly,
M. MCROY.

The report of Mr. Brown's escape spread far and wide, so that he was introduced to the Anti-Slavery Society in Philadelphia, from the office of which society a letter, of which the following is a copy, was written.

Anti-Slavery Office,
Philadelphia, April 8th, 1850.

H. Box BROWN,

My Dear Sir,—I was pleased to learn, by your letter, that it was your purpose to publish a narrative of the circumstances of your escape from slavery; such a publication, I should think, would not only be highly interesting, but well adapted to help on the cause of anti-slavery. Facts of this kind illustrate, without comment, the cruelty of the slave system, the fitness of its victims for freedom, and, at the same time, the guilt of the nation that tolerates its existence.

As one privy to many of the circumstances of your escape, *I* consider it one of the most remarkable exploits on record. That a man should come all the way from Richmond to Philadelphia, by the overland route, packed up in a box three feet long, by two and an half feet wide and deep, with scarcely a perceptible crevice for the admission of fresh air, and subject, at that time, to the rough handling and frequent shiftings of other freight, and that he should reach his destination alive, is a tale scarcely to be believed on the most irresistible testimony. I confess, if I had not myself been present at the opening of the box on its arrival, and had not witnessed with my own eyes, your resurrection from your living tomb, I should have been strongly disposed to question the truth of the story. As it was, however, seeing was believing, and believing was with me, at least, to be impressed with the diabolical character of

American Slavery, and the obligation that rests upon every one to labour for its overthrow.

Trusting that this may be the impression produced by your narrative, wherever it is read, and that it may be read wherever the evils of slavery are felt, I remain,

Your friend, truly,

J. MCKIM.

Were Mr. Brown in quest of an apology for publishing the following Narrative, the letter of Mr. McKim would form that apology. The Narrative was published in America, and an edition of 8,000 copies sold in about two months, such was the interest excited by the astounding revelations made by Mr. Brown as to the real character of slavery, and the hypocrisy of those professors of religion who have any connection with its infernal proceedings.

Several ministers of religion took a great interest in Mr. Brown, and did what they could to bring the subject of his escape properly before the public. The Rev. Mr. Spauldin, of Dover, N. H. was at the trouble to write to two of his brethren in the ministry, a letter, of which the following is a copy. The testimonials subjoining Mr. Spauldin's letter were given by persons who had witnessed the exhibition.

TO THE REV. MESSRS. PIKE AND BROOKS.
Dover, 12th July, 1850

DEAR BRETHREN,

A coloured gentleman, Mr. H. B. Brown, purposes to visit your village for the purpose of exhibiting his splendid PANORAMA or *Mirror of Slavery*. I have had the pleasure of seeing it, and am prepared to say, from what I have myself seen, and known in times past, of slavery and of the slave trade, in my opinion, it is almost, if not quite, a perfect fac simile of the workings of that horrible and fiendish system. The real *life-like* scenes presented in this PANORAMA, are admirably calculated to make an unfading impression upon the heart and memory, such as no lectures, books, or colloquial correspondence can produce, especially on the minds of children and young people, who should everywhere be brought before the altar of

Hannibal, to swear eternal hate to slavery, and love of rational freedom. If you can spare the time to witness the exhibition, I am quite certain you will feel yourselves amply rewarded. I know very well, there are a great many impostors and cheats going about through the country deceiving and picking up the people's money, but *this* is of another class altogether.

Yours, very truly,
JUSTIN SPAULDING.

I hereby certify that I have attended the exhibition of H. B. Brown's Panorama, in this village, with very deep interest; and most cordially subscribe my name, as an expression of my full concurrence with the sentiment of the recommendation above.

A. LATHAM

I agree cordially in the above testimonials.

A. CAVERNO.

I am not an experienced judge in paintings of this kind, but am only surprised that this is so well done and so much of it true to the life.

OLIVER AYER PORRER,
Of Franklin-street, Baptist Minister.
Dover, N.H. July 15th, 1850.

Although the following letter, as to date, should have occupied a place before the others, as it was addressed to the public and not to any particular person, its present position will answer every purpose of its publication.

Syracuse, April 26th, 1850.

To THE PUBLIC,
There are few facts, connected with the terrible history of American Slavery, that will be longer remembered, than that a

man escaped from the house of bondage, by coming from Richmond, Virginia, to Philadelphia, in a box *three feet, one inch long, two feet wide, and two feet six inches deep.* Twenty-seven hours he was closely packed within those small dimensions, and was tumbled along on drays, railroad cars, steam-boat, and horse carts, as any other box of merchandize would have been, sometimes on his feet, sometimes on his side, and once, for an hour or two, actually on his head.

Such is the well attested fact, and this volume contains the biography of the remarkable man, Henry Box Brown, who thus attained his freedom. Is there a man in our country, who better deserves his liberty? And is there to be found in these northern states, an individual base to assist in returning him to slavery! or to stand quietly by and consent to his re-capture?

The narrative of such a man cannot fail to be interesting, and I cordially commend it to all who love liberty and hate oppression.

SAMUEL J. MAY.

After Mr. Brown's arrival in the Free States and the recovery of his health, in addition to the publishing of his Narrative he began to prepare the Panorama, which has been exhibited with such success both in America and in England.

January, 1851.

We, the Teachers of St. John's Sunday School, Blackburn, having seen the exhibition in our School-room, called the "Panorama of American Slavery," feel it our duty to call upon all our Christian brethren, who may have an opportunity, to go and witness this great mirror of slavery for themselves, feeling assured ourselves that it is calculated to leave a lasting impression upon the mind, and particularly that of the young.

We recommend it more especially on account of the exhibitor, Mr. Henry Box Brown, being himself a fugitive saave, and therefore able to give a true account of all the horrors of American Slavery, together with his own miraculous escape.

Signed,

John Francis,	John Alston,
John Parkinson,	George Fielding,
Henry Ainsworth,	Thomas Higham,
John Tomlinson,	Daniel Tomlinson,
Henry Wilkinson,	Benjamin Cliff,
John Hartley,	John Howcutt,
James Greaves,	James Holt,
John Roberts,	Mark Shaw,
Francis Broughton,	Christopher Higham.

Mr. Brown continued to travel in the United States until the Fugitive Slave Bill—which passed into law last year—rendered it necessary for him to seek an asylum on British ground. Such was the vigilance with which the search for victims was pursued, that Mr. Brown had to travel under an assumed name, and by the most secret means shift his panorama to prevent suspicion and capture.

THOMAS G. LEE,
Minister of New Windsor Chapel, Salford.
April 8, 1851.

CHAPTER I

I was born about forty-five miles from the city of Richmond, in Louisa County, in the year 1815. I entered the world a slave—in the midst of a country whose most honoured writings declare that all men have a right to liberty—but had imprinted upon my body no mark which could be made to signify that my destiny was to be that of a bondman. Neither was there any angel stood by, at the hour of my birth, to hand my body over, by the authority of heaven, to be the property of a fellow-man; no, but I was a slave because my countrymen had made it lawful, in utter contempt of the declared will of heaven, for the strong to lay hold of the weak and to buy and to sell them as marketable goods. Thus was I born a slave; tyrants—remorseless, destitute of religion and every principle of humanity—stood by the couch of my mother and as I entered into the world, before I had done anything to forfeit my right to liberty, and while my soul was yet undefiled by the commission of actual sin, stretched forth their bloody arms and branded me with the mark of bondage, and by such means I became their own property. Yes, they robbed me of myself before I could know the nature of their wicked arts, and ever afterwards—until I forcibly wrenched myself from their hands—did they retain their stolen property.

My father and mother of course, were then slaves, but both of them are now enjoying such a measure of liberty, as the law affords to those who have made recompense to the tyrant for the right of property he holds in his fellow-man. It was not my fortune to be long under my mother's care; but I still possess a vivid recollection of her affectionate oversight. Such lessons as the following she would frequently give me. She would take me upon her knee and, pointing to the forest trees which were then stripped of their foliage by the winds of autumn, would say to me, my son, as yonder leaves

11

are stripped from off the trees of the forest, so are the children of the slaves swept away from them by the hands of cruel tyrants; and her voice would tremble and she would seem almost choked with her deep emotion, while the tears would find their way down her saddened cheeks. On those occasions she fondly pressed me to her heaving bosom, as if to save me from so dreaded a calamity, or to feast on the enjoyments of maternal feeling while she yet retained possession of her child. I was then young, but I well recollect the sadness of her countenance, and the mournful sacredness of her words as they impressed themselves upon my youthful mind— never to be forgotten.

Mothers of the North! as you gaze upon the fair forms of your idolised little ones, just pause for a moment; how would you feel if you knew that at any time the will of a tyrant—who neither could nor would sympathise with your domestic feelings — might separate them for ever from your embrace, not to be laid in the silent grave "where the wicked cease from troubling and where the weary are at rest," but to live under the dominion of tyrants and avaricious men, whose cold hearts cannot sympathise with your feelings, but who will mock at any manifestation of tenderness, and scourge them to satisfy the cruelty of their own disposition; yet such is the condition of hundreds of thousands of mothers in the southern states of America.

My mother used to instruct me in the principles of morality according to her own notion of what was good and pure; but I had no means of acquiring proper conception of religion in a state of slavery, where all those who professed to be followers of Jesus Christ evinced more of the disposition of demons than of men; and it is really a matter of wonder to me now, considering the character of my position that I did not imbibe a strong and lasting hatred of every thing pertaining to the religion of Christ. My lessons in morality were of the most simple kind. I was told not to steal, not to tell lies, and to behave myself in a becoming manner towards everybody. My mother, although a slave, took great delight in watching the result of her moral training in the character of my brother and myself, whilst—whether successful or unsuccessful in the formation of superior habits in us it is not for me to say—there were sown for her a blissful remembrance in the minds of her children, which will be cherished, both by the bond and the free, as long as life shall last.

As a specimen of the religious knowledge of the slave, I may here state what were my impressions in regard to my master; assuring the reader that I am not joking but stating what were the opinions of all the slaves' children on my master's plantation, so that some judgment may be formed of the care which was taken of our religious instruction. I really believed my old master was Almighty God, and that the young master was Jesus Christ! The reason of this error seems to have been that we were taught to believe thunder to be the voice of God, and when it was about to thunder my old master would approach us, if we were in the yard, and say, all you children run into the house now, for it is going to thunder; and after the thunder storm was over he would approach us smilingly and say "what a fine shower we have had," and bidding us look at the flowers would observe how prettily they appeared; we children seeing this so frequently, could not avoid the idea that it was he that thundered and made the rain to fall, in order to make his flowers look beautiful, and I was nearly my eight years of age before I got rid of this childish superstition. Our master was uncommonly kind (for even a slaveholder may be kind) and as he moved about in his dignity he seemed like a god to us, but not withstanding his kindness although he knew very well what superstitious notions we formed of him, he never made the least attempt to correct our erroneous impression, but rather seemed pleased with the reverential feelings which we entertained towards him. All the young slaves called his son saviour and the manner in which I was undeceived was as follows.—One Sabbath after preaching time my mother told my father of a woman who wished to join the church. She had told the preacher that she had been baptised by one of the slaves at night— a practice which is quite common. After they went from their work to the minister he asked her if she believed that our Saviour came into the world and had died for the sins of men? And she said "yes." I was listening anxiously to the conversation, and when my mother had finished, I asked her if my young master was not the saviour whom the woman said was dead? She said he was not, but it was our Saviour in heaven. I then asked her if there was a saviour there too; when she told me that young master was not our Saviour;— which astonished me very much. I then asked her if old master was not he? to which she replied he was not, and began to instruct me more fully in reference to the God of heaven. After this I believed there was a God who ruled the world, but I did not previously

CHAPTER II

My brother and myself were in the habit of carrying grain to the mill a few times in the year, which was the means of furnishing us with some information respecting other slaves, otherwise we would have known nothing whatever of what was going on anywhere in the world, expecting on our master's plantation. The mill was situated at a distance of about twenty miles from our residence, and belonged to one Colonel Ambler, in Yansinville county. On these occasions we used to acquire some little knowledge of what was going on around us, and we neglected no opportunity of making ourselves acquainted with the condition of other slaves.

On one occasion, while waiting for grain, we entered a house in the neighborhood, and while resting ourselves there, we saw a number of forlorn looking beings pass the door, and as they passed we noticed they gazed earnestly upon us; afterwards about fifty did the very same, and we heard some of them remarking that we had shoes, vests, and hats. We felt a desire to talk with them, and, accordingly after receiving some bread and meat from the mistress of the house we followed those abject beings to their quarters, and such a sight we had never witnessed before, as we had always lived on our master's plantation, and this was the first of our journeys to the mill. These Slaves were dressed in shirts made of coarse bagging such as coffee sacks are made from, and some kind of light substance for pantaloons, and this was all their clothing! They had no shoes, hats, vests, or coats, and when my brother spoke of their poor clothing they said they had never before seen colored persons dressed as we were; they looked very hungry, and we divided our bread and meat among them. They said they never had any meat given them by their master. My brother put various questions to them, such as if they had wives? did they go to church? &c., they said they had wives, but were obliged to marry persons who worked on the same plantation, as the master would not allow them to take wives from other plantations, consequently they were all related to each other, and the master obliged them to marry their relatives or to remain single. My brother asked one of them to show him his sister:—he said he could not distinguish them from the rest, as they were all his sisters. Although the slaves themselves entertain considerable respect for the law of marriage as a moral principle, and are exceedingly well pleased when they can obtain the services of a minister in the performance of the ceremony, yet the law recognizes no right in slaves to marry at all. The relation of husband and wife, parent and child, only exists by the toleration of their master, who may insult the slave's wife, or violate her person at any moment, and there is no law to punish him for what he has done. Now this not only may be as I have said, but it actually is the case to an alarming extent; and it is my candid opinion, that one of the strongest motives which operate upon the slave-holders in inducing them to maintain their iron grasp upon the unfortunate slaves, is because it gives them such unlimited control over the person of their female slaves. The greater part of slave-holders are licentious men, and the most respectable and kind masters keep some of these slaves as mistresses. It is for their pecuniary interest to do so, as their progeny is equal to so many dollars and cents in their pockets, instead of being a source of expense to them, as would be the case, if their slaves were free. It is a horrible idea, but it is no less true, that no slave husband has any certainty whatever of being able to retain his wife a single hour; neither has any wife any more certainty of her husband their fondest affection may be utterly disregarded, and their devoted attachment cruelly ignored at any moment a brutal slave-holder may think fit.

The slaves on Col. Ambler's plantation were never allowed to attend church, but were left to manage their religious affairs in their own way. An old slave whom they called John, decided on their religious profession and would baptize the approved parties during the silent watches of the night, while their master was asleep. We might have got information on many things from these slaves of Col. Ambler, but, while we were thus engaged, we perceived the overseer directing his steps towards us like a bear for its prey: we had however, time to ask one of them if they were ever whipped? to which he replied that not a day passed over their heads without some of them being brutally punished; "and" said he "we shall have to suffer for this talk with you. It was but this morning," he continued, "that many of us were severely whipped for having been baptized the night before!" After we left them we heard the screams of these poor creatures while they were suffering under the blows of the hard treatment received from the overseers, for the crime, as we supposed, of talking with us. We felt thankful that we were exempted from such treatment, but we had no certainty that we should not, ere long be placed in a similar position.

On returning to the mill we met a young man, a relation of the owner of this plantation, who for some time had been eyeing us very attentively. He at length asked us if we had ever been whipped? and when I told him we had not, he replied, "well neither of you will ever be of any value." He expressed a good deal of surprise that we were allowed to wear hats and shoes, supposing that slaves had no business to wear such clothing as their master wore. We had carried our fishing lines with us and requested the privilege of fishing in his stream, which he roughly denied us, saying "we do not allow niggers to fish." Nothing daunted, however, by the rebuff, my brother went to another place, where, without asking permission of any one, he succeeded in obtaining a plentiful supply of fish and on returning, the young slave-holder seemed to be displeased at our success, but, knowing that we caught them in a stream which was not under his control, he said nothing. He knew that our master was a rich slave-holder and, probably, he guessed from our appearance that we were favorites of his, so perhaps he was somewhat induced, from that consideration, to let us alone, at any rate he did not molest us any more.

We afterwards carried our corn to a mill belonging to a Mr. Bullock, only about ten miles distant from our plantation. This man was very kind to us; if we were late at night he would take us into his house, give us beds to sleep upon, and take charge of our horses. He would even carry our grain himself into the mill; and he always furnished us in the morning with a good breakfast. We were rather astonished, for some time, that this man was so kind to us—and, in this respect, so different from the other miller—until we learned that he was not a slave-holder. This miller allowed us to catch as many fishes as we chose, and even furnished us with fishing implements when we had money for only very imperfect ones, of our own.

While at this mill we became acquainted with a coloured man from a northern part of the country; and as our desire was strong to learn how our brethren fared in other places, we questioned him respecting his treatment. He complained much of his hard fate; he said he had a wife and one child, and begged for some of our fish to carry to his wife, which we gladly gave him. He told us he had just sent a few hickory nuts to market for which he had received thirty-six cents, and that he had given the money to his wife, to furnish her with some little articles of comfort.

On our return from their place, one time, we met with a coloured man and woman, who were very cross to each other. We inquired as to the cause of their disagreement and the man told us that the woman had such a tongue, and that some of them and taken a sheep because they did not get enough to eat, and this woman, after eating of it, went and told their master, and they had all received a severe whipping. This man enjoined upon his slaves never to steal from him again, but to steal as much as they chose from any other person: and if they took care to do it in such a manner, as the owner could not catch them in the act, nor be able to swear to the property after they had fetched it, he would shield them from punishment provided they would give him a share of the meat. Not long after this the slaves availing themselves of their master's protection, stole a pig from a neighbouring plantation, and, according to their agreement, furnished their master with his share. The owner of the missing animal, however, having heard something to make him suspect what had become of his property, came rushing into the house of the man who had just eaten of the stolen food, and in a very excited manner demanded reparation from him for the beast which his slaves had stolen; and the villain, rising from the table where he had just been eating of the stolen property, said, my servants know no more about your stolen hog than I do, which indeed was perfectly true, and the loser of the swine went away without saying any more; but although the master of this slave with whom we were talking, had told him that it was no sin to steal from others, my brother took good care to let him know, before we separated, that it was as much a sin in the sight of God to steal from the one as the other, "Oh," said the master, "niggers has nothing to do with God," and indeed the whole feature of slavery is so utterly inconsistent with the principles of religion, reason, and humanity, that it is no wonder that the very mention of the word God grates upon the ear as if it typefied the degeneracy of this hellish system.

> Turn! great Ruler of the skies!
> Turn from their sins thy searching eyes;
> Nor let the offences of their hand,
> Within thy book recorded stand.
>
> There's not a sparrow or a worm
> O'erlooked in thy decrees,
> Thou raisest monarchs to a throne—
> They sink with equal ease.
>
> May Christ's example, all divine,
> To us a model prove!
> Like his, O God! our hearts incline,
> Our enemies to love!

tends to buoy up the spirit of the slave, under the pressure of his severe toils, more than another, it is the hope of future freedom: by this his heart is cheered and his soul is lighted up in the midst of the fearful scenes of agony and suffering which he has to endure. Occasionally, as some event approaches from which lie can calculate on a relaxation of his sufferings, his hope burns with a bright blaze; but most generally the mind of the slave is filled with gloomy apprehension of a still harder fate. I have known many slaves to labour unusually hard with the view of obtaining the price of their own redemption, and, after they paid for themselves over and over again, were—by the unprincipled tyranny and fiendish mockery of moral principle in which their barbarous masters delight to indulge — still refused what they had so fully paid for, and what they so ardently desired. Indeed a great many masters hold out to their slaves the object of purchasing their own freedom—in order to induce them to labor more—without at the same time, entertaining the slightest idea of ever fulfilling their promise.

On the death of my old master, his property was inherited by four sons, whose names were, Stronn, Charles, John, and William Barret; so the human as well as every other kind of property, came to be divided equally amongst these four sons, which division—as it separated me from my father and mother, my sister and brother, with whom I had hitherto been allowed to live—was the most severe trial to my feelings which I had ever endured. I was then only fifteen years of age, but it is as present in my mind as if but yesterday's sun had shone upon the dreadful exhibition. My mother was separated from her youngest child, and it was not till after she had begged most pitiously for its restoration, that she was allowed to give it one farewell embrace, before she had to let it go for ever. This kind of torture is a thousand fold more cruel and barbarous than the use of the lash which lacerates the back; the gashes which the whip, or the cow skin makes may heal, and the place which was marked, in a little while may cease to exhibit the signs of what it had endured, but the pangs which lacerate the soul in consequence of the forcible disruption of parent and the dearest family ties, only grow deeper and more piercing, as memory fetches from a greater distance the horrid acts by which they have been produced. And there is no doubt but they under the weighty infirmities of declining life, and the increasing force and vividness with which the mind retains the memoranda of the agonies of former years—which form so great a part of memory's possessions in the minds of most slaves—hurry thousands annually from off the stage of life.

Mother, my sister Jane, and myself, fell into the hands of William Barret. My sister Mary and her children went another way; Edward, another, and John and Lewis and my sister Robinnet another. William Barret took my sister Martha for his "keep Miss." It is a difficult thing to divide all the slaves on a plantation; for no person wishes for all children, or all old people; while both old, young, and middle aged have to be divided:—but the tyrant slaveholder regards not the social, or domestic feelings of the slave, and makes his division according to the *moneyed* value they possess, without giving the slightest consideration to the domestic or social ties by which the individuals are bound to each other; indeed their common expression is, that "niggers have no feelings."

My father and mother were left on the plantation; but I was taken to the city of Richmond, to work in a tobacco manufactory, owned by my old master's son William, who had received a special charge from his father to take good care of me, and which charge my new master endeavoured to perform. He told me if I would behave well he would take good care of me and give me money to spend; he talked so kindly to me that I determined I would exert myself to the utmost to please him, and do just as he wished me in every respect. He furnished me with a new suit of clothes, and gave me money to buy things to send to my mother. One day I overheard him telling the overseer that *his father had raised me*—that I was a smart boy and that he must never whip me. I tried exceedingly hard to perform what I thought was my duty, and escaped the lash almost entirely, although I often thought the overseer would have liked to have given me a whipping, but my master's orders, which he dared not altogether to set aside, were my defence; so under these circumstances my lot was comparatively easy.

Our overseer at that time was a coloured man, whose name was Wilson Gregory; he was generally considered a shrewd and sensible man, especially to be a man of colour; and after the orders which my master gave him concerning me, he used to treat me very kindly indeed, and gave me board and lodgings in his own house. Gregory acted as book keeper also to my master, and was much in favour with the merchants of the city and all who knew him; he instructed me how to judge of the qualities of tobacco, and with the view of making me a more proficient judge of that article, he advised me to learn to chew and to smoke which I therefore did.

About eighteen months after I came to the city of Richmond, an extraordinary occurrence took place which caused great excitement all over the town. I did not then know precisely what was the cause of this excitement, for I could get no satisfactory information from my master, only he said that some of the slaves had plotted to kill their owners. I have since learned that it was the famous Nat Turner's insurrection. Many slaves were whipped, hung, and cut down with the swords in the streets; and some that were found away from their quarters after dark, were shot; the whole city was in the utmost excitement, and the whites seemed terrified beyond measure, so true it is that the "wicked flee when no man pursueth." Great numbers of slaves were loaded with irons; some were half hung as it was termed—that is they were suspended from some tree with a rope about their necks, so adjusted as not quite to strangle them—and then they were pelted by men and boys with rotten eggs. This half hanging is a refined species of punishment peculiar to slaves! This insurrection took place some distance from the city, and was the occasion of the enacting of that law by which more than five slaves were forbidden to meet together unless they were at work; and also of that, for the silencing all coloured preachers. One of that class in our city, refused to obey the impious mandate, and in consequence of his refusal, was severely whipped. His religion was, however, found to be too deeply rooted for him to be silenced by any mere power of man, and consequently, no efforts could avail to extort from his lips, a promise that he would cease to proclaim the glad tidings of the gospel to his enslaved and perishing fellow-men.

I had now been about two years in Richmond city and not having, during that time, seen, and very seldom heard from, my mother, my feelings were very much tried by the separation which I had thus to endure. I missed severely her welcome smile when I returned from my daily task; no one seemed at that time to sympathise with me, and I began to feel, indeed, that I really was alone in the world; and worse than all, I could console myself with no hope, not even the most distant, that I should ever see my beloved parents again.

About this time Wilson Gregory, who was our overseer, died, and his place was supplied by a man named Stephen Bennett, who had a wooden leg; and who used to creep up behind the slaves to hear what they had to talk about in his absence; but his wooden leg generally betrayed him by coming into contact with something which would make a noise, and that would call the attention of the slaves to what he was about. He was a very mean man in all his ways, and was very much disliked by the slaves. He used to whip them, often, in a shameful manner. On one occasion I saw him take a slave, whose name was Pinkney, and make him take him off his shirt; he then tied his hands and gave him one hundred lashes on his bare back; and all this, because he lacked three pounds of his task, which was valued at six cents. I saw him do many other things which were equally cruel, but it would be useless to multiply instances here, as no rational being doubts that slavery, even in its mildest forms is a hard and cruel fate. Yet with all his barbarities and cruelties this man was generally reckoned a very sensible man on religious subjects, and he used to be frequently talking about things of that sort, but sometimes he spoke with very great levity indeed. He used to say that if he died and went to hell, he had enough of sense to fool the devil and get out. He did take his departure at last, to that bower, whence borne, no traveller returns, and whether well or ill prepared for the change, I will not say.

Bennet was followed as overseer, by one Henry Bedman, and he was the best that we had. He neither used the whip nor cheated the hands of what little they had to receive, and I am confident that he had more work done by equal numbers of hands, than had been done under any overseer either before or since his appointment to office. He possessed a much greater influence by his kindness than any overseer did by his lash. He was altogether a very good man; was very fond of sacred music, and used to ask me and some of the other slaves, who were working in the same room to sing for him—something "smart" as he used to say, which we were generally as well pleased to do, as he was to ask us: it was not our fate however to enjoy his kindness long, he too very soon died, and his death was looked upon as a misfortune by all who had been slaves under him.

ever seen in low mean trickery and artifice. He used to boast that by his shrewdness in managing the slaves, he made enough to support himself and family— and he had a very large family which I am sure consumed not less than one hundred dollars per annum— without touching one farthing of his own salary, which was fifteen hundred dollars per annum.

Mr. Allen used to rise very early in the morning, not that he might enjoy sweet communion with his own thoughts, or with his God; nor that he might further the *legitimate* interest of his master, but in order to look after matters which principally concerned himself; that was to rob his master and the poor slaves that were under his control, by every means in his power. His early rising was looked upon by our master as a token of great devotedness to his business; and as he was with-all very pious and a member of the Episcopalian Church, my master seemed to place great confidence in him. It was therefore no use for any of the workmen to complain to the master of anything the overseer did, for he would not listen to a word they said, but gave his sanction to his barbarous conduct in the fullest extent, no matter how tyrannical or unjust that conduct, or how cruel the punishments which he inflicted; so that that demon of an overseer was in reality our master.

As a specimen of Allen's cruelty I will mention the revolting case of a coloured man, who was frequently in the habit of singing. This man was taken sick, and although he had not made his appearance at the factory for two or three days, no notice was taken of him; no medicine was provided nor was there any physician employed to heal him. At the end of that time Allen ordered three men to go to the house of the invalid and fetch him to the factory; and of course, in a little while the sick man appeared; so feeble was he however from disease, that he was scarcely able to stand. Allen, notwithstanding, desired him to be stripped and his hands tied behind him; he was then tied to a large post and questioned about his singing; Allen told him that his singing consumed too much time, and that it hurt him very much, but that he was going to give him some medicine that would cure him; the poor trembling man made no reply and immediately the pious overseer Allen for no other crime than sickness, inflicted two-hundred lashes upon his bare back; and even this might probably have been but a small part of his punishment, had a not the poor man fainted away: and it was only then the blood-thirsty fiend ceased to apply the lash!

I witnessed this transaction myself, but I durst not venture to say that the tyrant was doing wrong, because I was a slave and any interferance on my part, would have led to a similar punishment upon myself. This poor man was sick for four weeks afterwards, during which time the weekly allowance, of seventy cents, for the hands to board themselves with, was withheld, and the poor man's wife had to support him in the best way she could, which in a land of slavery is no easy matter.

The advocates of slavery will sometimes tell us, that the slave is in better circumstances than he would be in a state of freedom, because he has a master to provide for him when he is sick; but even if this doctrine were true it would afford no argument whatever in favor of slavery; for no amount of kindness can be made the lawful price of any man's liberty, to infringe which is contrary to the laws of humanity and the decrees of God. But what is the real fact? In many instances the severe toils and exposures the slave has to endure at the will of his master, brings on his disease, and even then he is liable to the *lash for medicine,* and to live, or die by starvation as he may, without any support from his owner; for there is no law by which the master may be punished for his cruelty—by which he may be compelled to support his suffering slave.

My master knew all the circumstances of the case which I have just related, but he never interfered, nor even reproved the cruel overseer for what he had done; his motto was, Mr. Allen is always right, and so, right or wrong, whatever he did was law, and from his will there was no appeal.

I have before stated, that Mr. Allen was a very pious man— he was also a church member, but was much addicted to the habit of profane swearing—a vice which is, in slave countries, not at all uncommon in church members. He used particularly to expend his swearing breath in denunciation of the whole race of negroes— using more bad terms than I could here employ, without polluting the pen with which I write. Amongst the best epithets, were; "hogs," "dogs," "pigs," &c., &c.

At one time he was busily engaged in reading the bible, when a slave came in who had been about ten minutes behind his time— precious time! Allen depended upon the punctuality of his slaves, for the support of his family, in the manner previously noticed: his anxiety to provide for his household led him to indulge in a boisterous outbreak of anger; so that when the slave came in, he said, what are you so late for you black scamp? The poor man endeavoured to apologize for his lateness, but it was to no purpose. This professing Christian proceeded to try the effects of the Bible on the slave's body, and actually dealt him a heavy blow in the face with the sacred book! But that not answering his purpose, and the man standing silent, he caught up a stick, and beat him with that. The slave afterwards complained to the master of the overseer's conduct, but was told that Mr. Allen would not do anything wrong.

Amongst Mr. Allen's other religious offices, he held that of superintendant of the Sunday school, where he used to give frequent exhortations to the slaves' children, in reference to their duty to their master. He told them they must never disobey their master, nor lie, nor steal, for if they did any of these, they would be sure to go to hell. But notwithstanding the deceitfulness of his character, and the fiendishness of his disposition, he was not, himself, perfectly proof, against the influence of fear. One day it came on a heavy thunderstorm; the clouds lowered heavily, and darkness usurped the dominion of day—it was so dark that the hands could not see to work, and I then began to converse with Mr. Allen about the storm. I asked him if it was not dangerous for the hands to work while the lightning flashed so terribly? He replied, he thought so, but he was placed there to keep them at their work, and he could not do otherwise. Just as we were speaking, a flash of lightning appeared to pass so close to us, that Mr. Allen jumped up from where he was sitting, and ran and locked himself up in a small room, where he supposed the lightning would not harm him. Some of the slaves said, they heard him praying that God would spare his life. That was a very severe storm, and a little while afterwards, we heard that a woman had been killed by the lightning. Although in the thunderstorm alluded to, Mr. Allen seemed to be alarmed; at other times he did not appear to think seriously about such things, for I have heard him say, that he did not think God had anything to do with thunder and lightning. This same official had much apparent zeal in the cause of the Sunday school; he used to pray with, and for the children, and was indefatigable in teaching them the catechism after him; he was very particular, however, in not allowing them to hold the book in their own hands. His zeal did not appear to have any higher object than that of making the children more willing slaves; for he used frequently to tell his visitors that coloured people were never converted—that they had no souls, and could not go to heaven, but it was his duty to talk to them as he did! His liberality to the white people, was coextensive with his denunciation of the coloured race; he said a white man may do what he pleased, and he could not be lost; he might lie, and rob the slaves, and do anything else, provided he read the bible and joined the church!

CHAPTER V

It may now be proper to say a little about the state of the churches in slave countries. There was a baptist minister in the city of Richmond, whose name was John Cave. I have heard this man declare in public, that he had preached six years before he was converted and the reason of his conversion was as follows.

He was in the habit of taking his glass of mint julep directly after prayers, or after preaching, which he thought wonderfully refreshed his soul and body; he would repeat the dram three or four times during the day. But an old slave of his, who had observed his practice hinted to him something about alternately drinking and preaching to the people; and, after thinking seriously on what the slave told him, he began to repent, and was converted. And now, he says he is truly converted, because his conscience reproved him for having made human beings articles of traffic; but I believe his second conversion is just about as complete as his first, for although he owed the second change to one of his own slaves, and ever confessed that the first effect of his conversion, was, to open up to his conscience the evil of the traffic in human beings, instead of letting those at liberty which he had under his control—and which might have been at once expected, as a natural consequence of his conviction— he endeavoured to apologize for the want of conscience, by finding, what he called, a good master for them, and selling them all to him.

But the religion of the slave-holder is everywhere a system of mere delusion, got up expressly for the purpose of deceiving the poor slaves, for everywhere the leading doctrine in the slaveholders' religion is, that it is the duty of the slave to obey his master in all things.

When Mr Carr left the city he was succeeded by a Mr. Jeter, who remained for many years; but at the time when he commenced his ministerial duties, many of the slaves were running away to free states; on the learning of which Mr. Jeter's first object was to devise some plan by which the masters could more effectively prevent their negroes from escaping; and the result of his ingenuity was as follows. He got the deacons and many more of the good Christians of his church, whether to believe or not I do not know, but to hold out that the place of meeting which they then occupyed was not large enough for them; and he seemed not to relish being in the same church with the negroes, but, however that was, he managed, with the assistance of his church members, to get the negroes all around the district to believe that out of love for them, and from pure regard to their spiritual interests, it had been agreed that the old meeting house was to be given to the negroes for their own use, on their paying a small portion of the price at which it was estimated. The church was valued at 13,000 dollars, but they would only be required to pay 3,000 dollars in order to have it for themselves. The negroes were pleased with the idea of having a place of meeting for themselves, and so were induced to save every cent they could to buy the chapel. They were thus provided with a strong motive for remaining where they were, and also by means of this pious fraud, which it afterwards proved itself to be, they were deprived of such little sums of money as might occasionally drop into their hands, and with which they might have been assisted in effecting their escape. These resolutions were punctually carried into effect; a splendid new church was built for the whites; and it was made a rule of that church, that if any coloured person entered it, without special business, he was liable to be taken to the watch-house and to receive thirty-nine lashes! The negroes paid what was at first demanded of them for the old building, but when they wished to get it placed entirely in their hands, they were charged with a still further sum; and after they had paid that, they had still more to pay, and never, so long as I was there, got possession of the church, and probably never will. A minister was, however, appointed to preach for them beside the one that preached for the white people.

A man named Knopp who came from the north preached once in the church of the negroes. He took for his text, *"O! Jerusalem, Jerusalem which killest the prophets and stonest them that are sent unto thee, how often would I have gathered thee as a hen gathereth her chidkens under her wings, and ye would not."* Mr. Jeter and the members of the whites' church were so offended at this man's sermon, that they went in a body to his lodgings and were about to mob him, if he had not been defended by a number of his own friends, but I believe if he had been left to the tender mercies of this professed servant of the Most High, and his Christian associates, he would never have escaped with his life.

The Rev. R. Ryland, who preached for the coloured people, was professor at the Baptist seminary near the city of Richmond, and the coloured people had to pay him a salary of 700 dollars per annum, although they neither chose him nor had the least control over him. He did not consider himself bound to preach regularly, but only when he was not otherwise engaged, so he preached about forty sermons a year and was a zealous supporter of the slave-holders' cause; and, so far as I could judge, he had no notion whatever of the pure religion of Jesus Christ. He used to preach from such texts as that in the epistle to the Ephesians, where St. Paul says, "servants be obedient to them that are your masters and mistresses according to the flesh, and submit to them with fear and trembling"; he was not ashamed to invoke the authority of heaven in support of the slave degrading laws under which masters could with impunity abuse their fellow-creatures.

because she did not do her duty, but because, it was said, her manners were too refined for a slave. At this time my wife had a child and this vexed Mrs. Colquitt very much; she could not bear to see her nursing her baby and used to wish some great calamity to happen to my wife. Eventually she was so much displeased with my wife that she induced Mr. Colquitt to sell her to one Philip M. Tabb, Junr. for the sum of 450 dollars; but coming to see the value of her more clearly after she tried to do without her, she could not rest till she got Mr. Colquitt to repurchase her from Mr. Tabb, which he did in about four months after he had sold her, for 500 dollars, being fifty more than he had sold her for.

Shortly after this Mr. Colquitt was taken sick, and his minister, the Rev. Dr. Plummer, was sent for to visit him; the doctor came and prayed for him and so did other members of the church; but he did not get any better so that they all thought he must soon die; the doctors had given up all hopes of him, and his wife and children, and friends, stood round his bedside in tears, expecting every minute he would breathe his last. All the servants were in readiness lest they should be called to go on some message. I had just then got home from labouring for my master; my wife was waiting for me, but she said she expected, every minute, that some person would be calling to tell her that master was gone, when, to my surprise, Joseph Colquitt sent to my wife to tell me to come and speak with him. I immediately left my room and went to his bed-side; and as soon as he saw me he caught hold of my hand and said;—"Henry will you pray for me and ask the Lord to spare my life, and restore me to health?" I felt it my duty to do the best I could in asking the Lord to have mercy upon him, because, although he was a slave-holder, and a very cruel man, and had used my wife very badly, yet I had no right to judge between him and his God, so I knelt down by his bed-side and prayed for him. After I got up he caught hold of my arm again and said, "one more favour I have to ask of you—go and tell all my slaves that belong to the church to come and pray for me." I went, according to his request, and we prayed three nights with him, after our work was done, and although we needed rest ourselves, yet at the earnest desire of the apparently dying man we were induced to forego our rest, and to spend our time in comforting him. At the end of this time he began to get a little better, and in a few weeks he was able to sit at table, and to take his meals with the family. I happened to be at his house one day, at our breakfast hour, after he got quite well, and his wife appeared as if she wished to joke her husband about the coloured people praying for him when he was sick. Mr. Colquitt had been expelled from the baptist church, and since that time she had disliked religion. She pretended that she did not believe either in God or Devil, and went on at such a rate, plaguing Mr. Colquitt, about the negroes praying for him, that he grew angry at last and exclaimed with an oath that it was all lies about the negroes praying for him; he denied asking any person to pray for him, and he said if he did ask the negroes to pray for him he must have been out of his senses, and did not, at the time he spoke, remember anything about it; but his wife still persisting in what she said, he went to the back door and calling his slaves one at a time, asked them who it was that prayed for him, until he got the names of all those who had been concerned in the affair, and when he had done so, he whipped every one of them which said he had prayed as Mrs. Colquitt had stated. He seemed wishful to whip me also, but, as I did not belong to him, he was deprived of the pleasure of paying me for my services in the manner, in which others had been rewarded. Mr. Colquitt, however, determined that I should suffer too, and for that purpose he proceeded to sell my wife to one Samuel Cottrell, who wished to purchase her. Cottrell was a saddler and had a shop in Richmond. This man came to me one day and told me that Mr. Colquitt was going to sell my wife and stated that he wanted a woman to wait upon his wife, and he thought my wife would precisely suit her; but he said her master asked 650 dollars for her and her children, and he had only 600 that he could conveniently spare but if I would let him have fifty, to make up the price, he would prevent her from being sold away from me. I was, however, a little suspicious about being fooled out of my money, and I asked him if I did advance the money what security I could have that he would not sell my wife as the others had done; but he said to me "do you think if you allow me to have that money, that I could have the heart to sell your wife to any other person but yourself, and particularly knowing that your wife is my sister and you my brother in the Lord; while all of us are members of the church? *Oh! no,* I never could have the heart to do such a deed as that." After he had shown off his religion in this manner, and lavished it upon me, I thought I would let him have the money, not that I had implicit faith in his promise, but that I knew he could purchase her if he wished whether I were to assist him or not, and I thought by thus bringing him under an obligation to me it might at least be somewhat to the advantage of my wife and to me; so I gave him the fifty dollars and he went off and bought my wife and children:—and that very same day he came to me and told me, that my wife and children were now his property, and that I must hire a house for them and he would allow them to live there if I would furnish them with everything they wanted, and pay him fifty dollars, a year; "if you don't do this," he said, "I will sell her as soon as I can get a buyer for her." I was struck with astonishment to think that this man, in one day, could exhibit himself in two such different characters. A few hours ago filled with expressions of love and kindness, and now a monster tyrant, making light of the most social ties and imposing such terms as he chose on those whom, but a little, before, he had begged to conform to his will. Now, being a slave, I had no power to hire a house, and what this might have resulted in I do not know, if I had not met with a friend in the time of need, in the person of James C. A. Smith, Jr. He was a free man and I went to him and told him my tale and asked him to go and hire a house for me, to put my wife and children into; which he immediately did. He hired one at seventy-two dollars per annum, and stood master of it for me; and, notwithstanding the fearful liabilities under which I lay, I now began to feel a little easier, and might, perhaps, have managed to live in a kind of a way if we had been let alone here. But Mr. S. Cottrell had not yet done with robbing us; he no sooner saw that we were thus comfortably situated, than he said my wife must do some of his washing. I still had to pay the house hire, and the hire of my wife; to find her and the children with everything they required, and she had to do his washing beside. Still we felt ourselves more comfortable than we had ever been before. In this way, we went on for some time: I paid him the hire of my wife regularly, whenever he called for it—whether it was due or not—but he seemed still bent on robbing me more thoroughly than he had the previous day; for one pleasant morning, in the month of August, 1848, when my wife and children, and myself, were sitting at table, about to eat our breakfast, Mr. Cottrel called, and said, he wanted some money to day, as he had a demand for a large amount. I said to him, you know I have no money to spare, because it takes nearly all that I make for myself, to pay my wife's hire, the rent of my house, my own ties to my master, and to keep ourselves in meat and clothes; and if at any time, I have made any thing more than that, I have paid it to you in advance, and what more can I do? Mr. Cottrell, however said, "I want money, and money I will have." I could make him no answer; he then went away. I then said to my wife "I wonder what Mr. Cottrell means by saying I want money and money I will have," my poor wife burst into tears and said perhaps he will sell one of our little children, and our hearts were so full that neither of us could eat any breakfast, and after mutually embracing each other, as it might be our last meeting, and fondly pressing our little darlings to our bosoms, I left the house and went off to my daily labour followed by my little children who called after me to come back soon. I felt that life had joys worth living for if I could only be allowed to enjoy them, but my heart was filled with deep anguish from the awful calamity, which I was thus obliged to contemplate, as not only a possible but a highly probable occurrence. I now went away to my work and I could as I went see many other slaves hastening in the same direction. I began to consider their lot and mine, and although my heart was filled with sorrow I felt still disposed to look upon the bright side of the future. I could still see some alleviation to my case of sorrow; it was true that the greater portion of my earnings were stolen from me by the unscrupulous hand of my master; that I was entirely at his mercy; and might at any moment be snatched from those enjoyments as well as those I thought were open to me; that if he chose he might still further gratify his robbing propensities and demand a larger portion of my earnings; so that the pleasures of intellect would be completely closed to my mind, but I could enjoy myself with my family about me while I listened to the pleasing prattle of my children, and experience the kindness of a wife, which were privileges that every slave could not enjoy.

I had not been many hours at my work, when I was informed that my wife and children were taken from their home, sent to the auction mart and sold, and then lay in prison ready to start away the next day for North Carolina with the man who had purchased them. I cannot express, in language, what were my feelings on this occasion. My master treated me kindly but he still retained me in a state of slavery. His kindness however did not keep me from feeling the smart of this awful deprivation. I had left my wife and children at home in the morning as well situated as slaves could be; I was not anticipating their loss, not on account of the feigned piety of their owner, for I had long ago learned to look through such hollow pretences in those who held slaves, but because of the obligation to me for money I had advanced to him, *on the expressed condition that he should not sell her to any person but myself;* such, however was the case, and as soon as I could get away, I went and purchased some things to take to the jail to them I so much loved; and to have one farewell embrace before parting for ever. I had not proceeded far however when I met with a gentleman who perceiving my anguish of heart, as depicted in my countenance, inquired what was the matter with me. I had no sooner hinted at my circumstances, however, than he knew all about it, having heard it, before. He advised me not to go to the jail, "for" said he "the man that bought your wife and family has told your master some falsehoods and has ordered the jailor to seize you and put you in prison if you should make your appearance there; when you would most likely be sold separately from them, because the *Methodist Minister* that bought your wife, does not want any men," so being thus advised I thought it better not to go to the jail myself, but I procured a friend to go in my stead, and take some money and the things which I had purchased for my wife, and tell her how it was that I could not come myself. And it turned out in the end to be much better that I did not go, for as soon as the young man arrived at the jail he was seized and put in prison, the jailor mistaking him for me: but when he discovered his mistake he was very angry and vented his rage upon the innocent youth by kicking him out of the prison. He discovered his mistake by asking my wife if that were not her husband, she said he was not; but he was not satisfied with her answer for he asked the children also if he were not their father, and as they too said no he was convinced, and then proceeded to abuse the young man in the manner before mentioned.

After I had heard of these things, I went to my *Christian* master and informed him how I was served, but he shoved me away from him as if I was not human. I could not rest with this however, I went to him a second time and implored him to be kind enough to buy my wife and to save me from so much trouble of mind; still he was inexorable and only answered me by telling me to go to my work and not bother him any more. I went to him a *third* time, which would be about ten o'clock and told him how Cottrell had robbed me, as this scoundrel was not satisfied with selling my wife and children, but he had no sooner got them out of the town than he took everything which he could find in my house and carried it off to be sold; the things which he then took had cost me nearly three hundred dollars. I begged master to write Cottrell and make him give me up my things, but his answer was Mr. Cottrell is a gentleman I am afraid to meddle with his business. So having satisfied myself that the master would do nothing for me, I left him and went to two young gentlemen with whom I was acquainted to try if I could induce them to buy my wife; but when I had stated my case to them they gave me to understand that they did not deal in slaves so they could not do that, but they expressed their willingness to do anything else that I might desire of them; so finding myself unsuccessful here, I went sorrowfully back to my own deserted home and found that what I had heard was quite true; not only had my wife and children been taken away, but every article of furniture had also been removed to the auction mart to be sold. I then made inquiry as to where my things had been put; and having found this out went to the sherriff's office and informed him, that the things Mr. Cottrell had brought to be sold did not belong to him, but that they were mine, and I hoped he would return them to me. I was then told by the sherriff that Mr. Cottrell had left the things to be sold in order to pay himself a debt of seventeen dollars and twenty-one cents, which he said if I would pay he would let me take away the things. I then went to my good friend Doctor Smith who was always ready and willing to do what he could for me, and having got the money, I paid it to the sherriff and took away the things which I was obliged to do that night, as far as I was able, and what were left I removed in the morning. When I was taking home the last of my things I met Mr. Cottrell, and two of his Christian brethren, in the street. He stopped me and said he had heard I had been to the sherriff's office and got away my things. Yes I said I have been and got away *my things* but I could not get away *my wife and children* whom you have put beyond my power to redeem. He then began to give me a round of abuse, while his two Christian friends stood by and heard him, but they did not seem to be the least offended at the terrible barbarity which was there placed before them.

I now left Mr. Cottrell and his friends, and going home, endeavored to court a little rest by lying down in a position so as to induce sleep. I had borne too heavy a load of grief on my mind to admit of me even closing my eyes for an hour during the whole night. Many schemes for effecting the redemption of my family passed through my mind, but when the morning's sun arose I found myself on my way towards my master's house, to make another attempt to induce him to purchase my wife. But although I besought him, with tears in my eyes, I did not succeed in making the least impression on his obdurate heart, and he utterly refused to advance the smallest portion of the 5000 dollars I had paid him in order to relieve my sufferings, and yet he was a church member of considerable standing in Richmond. He even told me that I could get another wife and so I need not trouble myself about that one; but I told him those that God had joined together let no man put assunder, and that I did not want another wife, but my own whom I had loved so long. The mentioning of the passage of scripture seemed to give him much offence for he instantly drove me from his house saying he did not wish to hear that!

My agony was now complete, she with whom I had travelled the journey of life *in chains,* for the space of twelve years, and the dear little pledges God had given us I could see plainly must now be separated from me forever, and I must continue, desolate and alone, to drag my chains through the world. O dear, I thought, shall my wife and children no more greet my sight with their cheerful looks and happy smiles! for far away in the North Carolina swamps are they henceforth to toil beneath the scorching rays of a hot sun deprived of a husband's and a father's care! Can I endure such agony—shall I stay behind while they are thus driven with the tyrant's rod? I must stay, I am a slave, the law of men gives me no power to ameliorate my condition; it shuts up every avenue of hope; but, thanks be to God, there is a law of heaven which senates' laws cannot control!

While I was thus musing I received a message, that if I wished to see my wife and children, and bid them the last farewell, I could do so, by taking my stand on the street where they were all to pass on their way for North Carolina. I quickly availed myself of this information, and placed myself by the side of a street, and soon had the melancholy satisfaction of witnessing the approach of a gang of slaves, amounting to three hundred and fifty in number, marching under the direction of a Methodist minister, by whom they were purchased, and amongst which slaves were my wife and children. I stood in the midst of many who, like myself, were mourning the loss of friends and relations and had come there to obtain one parting look at those whose company they but a short time before had imagined they should always enjoy, but who were, without any regard to their own wills, now driven by the tyrant's voice and the smart of the whip on their way to another scene of toil, and, to them, another land of sorrow in a far off southern country. These beings were marched with ropes about their necks, and staples on their arms, and, although in that respect the scene was no very novel one to me, yet the peculiarity of my own circumstances made it assume the appearance of unusual horror. This train of beings was accompanied by a number of waggons loaded with little children of many different families, which as they appeared rent the air with their shrieks and cries and vain endeavours to resist the separation which was thus forced upon them, and the cords with which they were thus bound; but what should I now see in the very foremost wagon but a little child looking towards me and pitifully calling, father! father! This was my eldest child, and I was obliged to look upon it for the last time that I should, perhaps, ever see it again in life; if it had been going to the grave and this gloomy procession had been about to return its body to the dust from whence it sprang, whence its soul had taken its departure for the land of spirits, my grief would have been nothing in comparison to what I then felt; for then I could have reflected that its sufferings were over and that it would never again require nor look for a father's care; but now it goes with all those tender feelings riven, by which it was endeared to a father's love; it must still live subject to the deprivation of paternal care and to the chains and wrongs of slavery, and yet be dead to the pleasure of a father from whose heart the impression of its early innocence and love will never be effaced. Thus passed my child from my presence—it was my own child—I loved it with all the fondness of a father; but things were so ordered that I could only say, farewell, and leave it to pass in its chains while I looked for the approach of another gang in which my wife was also loaded with chains. My eye soon caught her precious face, but, gracious heavens! that glance of agony may God spare me from ever again enduring! My wife, under the influence of her feelings, jumped aside; I seized hold of her hand while my

CHAPTER VII

I had for a long while been a member of the choir in the Affeviar church in Richmond, but after the severe family affliction to which I have just alluded in the last chapter and the knowledge that these cruelties were perpetrated by ministers and church members, I began strongly to suspect the Christianity of the slave-holding church members and hesitated much about maintaining my connection with them. The suspicion of these slave-dealing Christians was the means of keeping me absent from all their churches from the time that my wife and children were torn from me, until Christmas day in the year 1848; and I would not have gone then but being a leading member of the choir, I yielded to the entreaties of my associates to assist at a concert of sacred music which was to be got up for the benefit of the church. My friend Dr. Smith, who was the conductor of the underground railway, was also a member of the choir, and when I had consented to attend he assisted me in selecting twenty-four pieces to be sung on the occasion.

On the day appointed for our concert I went along with Dr. Smith, and the singing commenced at half-past three o'clock, p.m. When we had sung about ten pieces and were engaged in singing the following verse—

> Again the day returns of holy rest,
> Which, when he made the world, Jehovah blest;
> When, like his own, he bade our labours cease,
> And all be piety, and all be peace,

the members were rather astonished at Dr. Smith, who stood on my right hand, suddenly closing his book, and sinking down upon his seat his eyes being at the same time filled with tears. Several of them began to inquire what was the matter with him, but he did not tell them. I guessed what it was and afterwards found out that I had judged of the circumstances correctly. Dr. Smith's feelings were overcome with a sense of doing wrongly in singing for the purpose of obtaining money to assist those who were buying and selling their fellow-men. He thought at that moment he felt reproved by Almighty God for lending his aid to the cause of slave-holding religion; and it was under this impression he closed his book and formed the resolution which he still acts upon, of never singing again or taking part in the services of a pro-slavery church. He is now in New England publicly advocating the cause of emancipation.

After we had sung several other pieces we commenced the anthem, which run thus—

> Vital spark of heavenly flame,
> Quit, O! quit the mortal frame,—

these words awakened in me feelings in which the sting of former sufferings was still sticking fast, and stimulated by the example of Dr. Smith, whose feelings I read so correctly, I too made up my mind that I would be no longer guilty of assisting those bloody dealers in the bodies and souls of men; and ever since that time I have steadfastly kept my resolution.

I now began to get weary of my bonds; and earnestly panted after liberty. I felt convinced that I should be acting in accordance with the will of God, if I could snap in sunder those bonds by which I was held body and soul as the property of a fellow man. I looked forward to the good time which every day I more and more firmly believed would yet come, when I should walk the face of the earth in full possession of all that freedom which the finger of God had so clearly written on the constitutions of man, and which was common to the human race; but of which, by the cruel hand of tyranny, I, and millions of my fellow-men, had been robbed.

I was well acquainted with a store-keeper in the city of Richmond, from whom I used to purchase my provisions; and having formed a favourable opinion of his integrity, one day in the course of a little conversation with him, I said to him if I were free I would be able to do business such as he was doing; he then told me that my occupation (a tobacconist) was a money-making one, and if I were free I had no need to change for another. I then told him my circumstances in regard to my master, having to pay him twenty-five dollars per month, and yet that he refused to assist me in saving my wife from being sold and taken away to the South, where I should never see her again; and even refused to allow me to go and see her until my hours of labour were over. I told him this took place about five months ago, and I had been meditating my escape from slavery since, and asked him, as no person was near us, if he could give me any information about how I should proceed. I told him I had a little money and if he would assist me I would pay him for so doing. The man asked me if I was not afraid to speak that way to him; I said no, for I imagined he believed that every man had a right to liberty. He said I was quite right, and asked me how much money I would give him if he would assist me to get away. I told him that I had 166 dollars and that I would give him the half; so we ultimately agreed that I should have his service in the attempt for eighty-six. Now I only wanted to fix upon a plan. He told me of several plans by which others had managed to effect their escape, but none of them exactly suited my taste. I then left him to think over what would be best to be done, and, in the mean time, went to consult my friend Dr. Smith, on the subject. I mentioned the plans which the store-keeper had suggested, and as he did not approve either of them very much, I still looked for some plan which would be more certain and more safe, but I was determined that come what may, I should have my freedom or die in the attempt.

One day, while I was at work, and my thoughts were eagerly feasting upon the idea of freedom, I felt my soul called out to heaven to breathe a prayer to Almighty God. I prayed fervently that he who seeth in secret and knew the inmost desires of my heart, would lend me his aid in bursting my fetters asunder, and in restoring me to the possession of those rights, of which men had robbed me; when the idea suddenly flashed across my mind of shutting myself *up in a box,* and getting myself conveyed as dry goods to a free state.

Being now satisfied that this was the plan for me, I went to my friend Dr. Smith and, having aquainted him with it, we agreed to have it put at once into execution not however without calculating the chances of danger with which it was attended; but buoyed up by the prospect of freedom and increased hatred to slavery I was willing to dare even death itself rather than endure any longer the clanking of those galling chains. It being still necessary to have the assistance of the store-keeper, to see that the box was kept in its right position on its passage, I then went to let him know my intention, but he said although he was willing to serve me in any way he could, he did not think I could live in a box for so long a time as would be necessary to convey me to Philadelphia, but as I had already made up my mind, he consented to acompany me and keep the box right all the way.

My next object was to procure a box, and with the assistance of a carpenter that was very soon accomplished, and taken to the place where the packing was to be performed. In the mean time the store-keeper had written to a friend in Philidelphia, but as no answer had arrived, we resolved to carry out our purpose as best we could. It was deemed necessary that I should get permission to be absent from my work for a few days, in order to keep down suspicion until I had once fairly started on the road to liberty; and as I had then a gathered finger I thought that would form a very good excuse for obtaining leave of absence; but when I showed it to one overseer, Mr. Allen, he told me it was not so bad as to prevent me from working, so with a view of making it bad enough, I got Dr. Smith to procure for me some oil of vitriol in order to drop a little of this on it, but in my hurry I dropped rather much and made it worse than there was any occasion for, in fact it was very soon eaten in to the bone, and on presenting it again to Mr. Allen I obtained the permission required, with the advice that I should go home and get a poultice of flax-meal to it, and keep it well poulticed until it got better. I took him instantly at his word and went off directly to the store-keeper who had by this time received an answer from his friend in Philadelphia, and had obtained permission to address the box to him, this friend in that city, arranging to call for it as soon as it should arrive. There being no time to be lost, the store-keeper, Dr. Smith, and myself, agreed to meet next morning at four o'clock, in order to get the box ready for the express train. The box which I had procured was three feet one inch wide, two feet six inches high, and two feet wide: and on the morning of the 29th day of March, 1849, I went into the box—having previously bored three gimlet holes opposite my face, for air, and provided myself with a bladder of water, both for the purpose of quenching my thirst and for wetting my face, should I feel getting faint. I took the gimlet also with me, in order that I might bore more holes if I found I had not sufficient air. Being thus equipped for the battle of liberty, my friends nailed down the lid and had me conveyed to the Express Office, which was about a mile distant from the place where I was packed. I had no sooner arrived at the office than I was turned heels up, while some person nailed something on the end of the box. I was then put upon a wagon and driven off to the depot with my head down, and I had no sooner arrived at the depot, than the man who drove the wagon tumbled me roughly into the baggage car, where, however, I happened to fall on my right side.

The next place we arrived at was Potomac Creek, where the baggage had to be removed from the cars, to be put on board the steamer; where I was again placed with my head down, and in this dreadful position had to remain nearly an hour and a half, which, from the sufferings I had thus to endure, seemed like an age to me, but I was forgetting the battle of liberty, and I was resolved to conquer or die. I felt my eyes swelling as if they would burst from their sockets; and the veins on my temples were dreadfully distended with pressure of blood upon my head. In this position I attempted to lift my hand to my face but I had no power to move it; I felt a cold sweat coming over me which seemed to be a warning that death was about to terminate my earthly miseries, but as I feared even that, less than slavery, I resolved to submit to the will of God, and, under the influence of that impression, I lifted up my soul in prayer to God, who alone, was able to deliver me. My cry was soon heard, for I could hear a man saying to another, that he had travelled a long way and had been standing there two hours, and he would like to get somewhat to sit down; so perceiving my box, standing on end, he threw it down and then two sat upon it. I was thus relieved from a state of agony which may be more easily imagined than described. I could now listen to the men talking, and heard one of them asking the other what he supposed *the box contained;* his companion replied he guessed it was "THE MAIL." I too thought it was a mail but not such a mail as he supposed it to be.

The next place at which we arrived was the city of Washington, where I was taken from the steam boat, and again placed upon a wagon and carried to the depot right side up with care; but when the driver arrived at the depot I heard him call for some person to help to take the box off the wagon, and someone answered him to the effect that he might throw it off; but, says the driver, it is marked "this side up with care"; so if I throw it off I might break something the other answered him that it did not matter if he broke all that was in it, the railway company were able enough to pay for it. No sooner were these words spoken than I began to tumble from the wagon, and falling on the end where my head was, I could hear my neck give a crack, as if it had been snapped asunder and I was knocked completely insensible. The first thing I heard, after that, was some person saying, "there is no room for the box, it will have to remain and be sent through to-morrow with the luggage train"; but the Lord had not quite forsaken me, for in answer to my earnest prayer. He so ordered affairs that I should not be left behind; and I now heard a man say that the box had come with the express, and it must be sent on. I was then tumbled into the car with my head downwards again, but the car had not proceeded far before, more luggage having to be taken in, my box got shifted about and so happened to turn upon its right side; and in this position I remained till I got to Philadelphia, of our arrival in which place I was informed by hearing some person say, "We are in port and at Philadelphia." My heart then leaped for joy, and I wondered if any person knew that such a box was there.

Here it may be proper to observe that the man who had promised to accompany my box failed to do what he promised; but, to prevent it remaining long at the station after its arrival, he sent a telegraphic message to his friend, and I was only twenty-seven hours in the box, though travelling a distance of three hundred and fifty miles.

I was now placed in the depot amongst the other luggage, where I lay till seven o'clock, P.M., at which time a wagon drove up, and I heard a person inquire for such a box as that in which I was. I was then placed on a wagon and conveyed to the house where my friend in Richmond had arranged. I should be received. A number of persons soon collected round the box after it was taken in to the house, but as I did not know what was going on I kept myself quiet. I heard a man say "let us rap upon the box and see if he is alive"; and immediately a rap ensued and a voice said, tremblingly, "Is all right within?" to which I replied—"all right." The joy of the friends was very great; when they heard that I was alive they soon managed to break open the box, and then came my resurrection from the grave of slavery. I rose a freeman, but I was too weak, by reason of long confinement in that box, to be able to stand, so I immediately swooned away. After my recovery from the swoon the first thing, which arrested my attention was the presence of a number of friends, every one seeming more anxious than another, to have an opportunity of rendering me their assistance, and of bidding me a hearty welcome to the possession of my natural rights, I had risen as it were from the dead; I felt much more than I could readily express; but as the kindness of Almighty God had been so conspicuously shown in my deliverance, I burst forth into the following hymn of thanksgiving,

I waited patiently, I waited patiently for the Lord, for the Lord;
And he inclined unto me, and heard my calling:
I waited patiently, I waited patiently for the Lord,
And he inclined unto me, and heard my calling:
And he hath put a new song in my mouth,
Even a thanksgiving, even a thanksgiving even a thanksgiving unto
    our God.
Blessed, Blessed, Blessed, Blessed is the man, Blessed is the man,
Blessed is the man that hath set his hope, his hope in the Lord;
O Lord my God, Great, Great, Great,

Great are the wondrous works which thou hast done.
Great are the wondrous works which thou hast done, which thou
    hast done:
If I should declare them and speak of them, they would be more,
    more, more, than I am able to express.
I have not kept back thy loving kindness and truth from the great
    congregation.
I have not kept back thy loving kindness and truth from the great
    congregation.
Withdraw not thou thy mercy from me,
Withdraw not thou thy mercy from me, O Lord;
Let thy loving kindness and thy truth always preserve me,
Let all those that seek thee be joyful and glad,
Let all those that seek thee be joyful and glad, be joyful, and glad,
    be joyful, be joyful, be joyful, be joyful, be joyful and glad—be
    glad in thee. And let such as love thy salvation,
And let such as love thy salvation, say, always,
The Lord be praised,

The Lord be praised.
Let all those that seek thee be joyful and glad,
And let such as love thy salvation, say always,
The Lord be praised,
The Lord be praised,
The Lord be praised.

    I was then taken by the hand and welcomed to the houses of the following friends—Mr. J. Miller, Mr. McKin, Mr. and Mrs. Motte, Mr. and Mrs. Davis, and many others, by all of whom I was treated in the kindest manner possible. But it was thought proper that I should not remain long in Philadelphia, so arrangements were made for me to proceed to Massachusetts, where, by the assistance of a few Anti-slavery friends, I was enabled shortly after to arrive. I went to New York, where I became acquainted with Mr. II. Long, and Mr. Eli Smith, who were very kind to me the whole time I remained there. My next journey was to New Bedford, where I remained some weeks under the care of Mr. II. Ricketson, my finger being still bad from the effects of the oil of vitriol with which I dressed it before I left Richmond. While I was here I heard of a great anti-slavery meeting which was to take place in Boston, and being anxious to identify myself with that public movement, I proceeded there and had the pleasure of meeting the hearty sympathy of thousands to whom I related the story of my escape. I have since attended large meetings in different towns in the states of Maine, New Hampshire, Vermont, Connecticut, Rhode Island, Pennsylvania, and New York, in all of which places I have found many friends and have endeavored, according to the best of my abilities, to advocate the cause of the emancipation of the slave; with what success I will not pretend to say—but with a daily increasing confidence in the humanity and justice of my cause, and in the assurance of the approbation of Almighty God.

    I have composed the following song in commemoration of my fete in the box:—

Air:—"Uncle Ned."

I

Here you see a man by the name of Henry Brown,

Run away from the South to the North;
Which he would not have done but they stole all his rights,
But they'll never do the like again.

> *Chorus*—Brown laid down the shovel and the hoe,
> Down in the box he did go;
> No more Slave work for Henry Box Brown,
> In the box *by Express* he did go

II

Then the orders they were given, and the cars did start away,
Roll along—roll along—roll along,
Down to the landing, where the steamboat lay,
To bear the baggage off to the north.
Chorus

III

When they packed the baggage on, they turned him on his head,
There poor Brown liked to have died;
There were passengers on board who wished to sit down,
And they turned the box down on its side.
Chorus

IV

When they got to the cars they threw the box off,
And down upon his head he did fall,
Then he heard his neck crack, and he thought it was broke,
But they never threw him off any more.
Chorus

V

When they got to Philadelphia they said he was in port,
And Brown then began to feel glad,
He was taken on the waggon to his final destination,
And left, "this side up with care."
Chorus

VI

The friends gathered round and asked if all was right,
As down on the box they did rap,
Brown answered them, saying, "yes all is right!"
He was then set free from his pain.

Chorus

proceeded to employ the Instruments which God had sent them, and ever since the colored race have had to labor with the shovel and the hoe, while the rich man works with the pen and ink!

I have no apology whatever to make for what I have said, in regard to the pretended Christianity under which I was trained, while a slave. I have felt it my duty to speak of it harshly; because I have felt its blasting influence, and seen it used as a cloak under which to conceal the most foul and wicked deeds. Indeed the only thing I think it necessary to say in this place is what seems to me, and what may really be matter of serious doubt to persons who have the privilege of living in a free country, under the influence of liberal institutions; that there actually does exist in that land where men, women, and children are bought and sold, a church, calling itself the church of Christ; yes, my friends, it is true that the buyer and seller of the bodies and souls of his fellows; he who to day, can separate the husband from the wife, the parent from the child, or cut asunder the strongest ties of friendship, in order to gain a few dollars, to avert a trifling loss, or to please a whim of fancy, can ascend a pulpit tomorrow and preach, what he calls the gospel of Christ! Yes, and in many cases, the house, which he calls the house of God, has been erected from the price of human beings; the very stones of which it is composed, have actually been dragged to their places by man with chains at their heels, and ropes about their neck! It is not for me to judge between those men and the God whom they pretend to serve, if their own consciences do not condemn them. I pray that God may give them light to see the error of their ways, and if they know that they are doing wrongly, that he may give them grace to renovate, their hearts!

A few specimens of the laws of a slave-holding people may not be out of place here; not that by such means, we can hope to convey a true idea of the actual condition of the people of these places, because those matters on which the happiness or misery of a people principally depend, and in general such matters as are entirely beyond the reach of law. Beside—the various circumstances, which, independent of the law, in civilised and free countries, constitute the principal sources of happiness or misery—in the slave-holding states of America, there is a strong current of public opinion which the law is altogether incompetent to control. In many cases there are ideas of criminality, which are not by statute law attached to the commission of certain acts, but which are frequently found to exist under the title of "Lynch law" either augmenting the punishment which the law requires, or awarding punishment to what the law does not recognize as crime—as the following will be sufficient to show.

"The letter of the law would have been sufficient for the protection of the lives of the miserable gamblers, in Vicksburg, and other places in Mississippi, from the rage of those whose money they had won; but gentlemen of property and standing, laughed the law to scorn, rushed to the gambler's houses, put ropes round their necks, dragged them through the streets, hanged them in the public square, and thus saved the money they had not yet paid. Thousands witnessed this wholesale murder, yet of the scores of legal officers present, not one raised a finger to prevent it. How many hundreds of them helped to commit the murder with their own hands, does not appear, but many of them has been indicted for it, and no one has made the least effort to bring them to trial. Now the laws of Mississippi were not in fault, when those men were murdered, nor were they in fault, that the murders were not punished; the law demanded it, but the people of Mississippi, the legal officers, the grand juries, and legislature of the state, with one consent determine that the law shall be a dead letter, and thus, the whole state assumes the guilt of these murders, and, in bravado, flourish their reeking hands in the face of the world; for the people of Vicksburg have actually erected a monument in honor of Dr. H. S. Bodley, who was the ring-leader of the Lynchers in this case."—*American Slavery as it is.*

It may be also worthy of remark, that in all cases in which we have strong manifestation of public opinion, in opposition to the law, it is always exhibited in the direction of cruelty; indeed, that such should be the case, no person intimately acquainted with the nature of the human mind, need be in the least surprised. Who can consider the influence which the relationship of master and slave— so extensively subsisting between the members of slave states—in stimulating the passion and in degrading the moral feelings, without being prepared to credit all that is said of slavery? The most perfect abstract of the laws which regulate the duties of slaves and slave-owners, must doubtless fail to convey any proper idea of the actual state of the slave; and the few laws which we here cite, are not given for that purpose, but as a sample of trash, which is called justice by slave-holders and quasi legal authorities.

"All negroes, mulattoes, or mertizoes, who now are, or shall hereafter, be in this province, and all their offspring, are hereby declared to be, and shall remain for ever hereafter, absolute slaves, and shall follow the condition of the mother."—*Law of South Carolina.*

"The criminal offence of assault and battery, cannot, at common law, be committed upon the person of a slave, for, notwithstanding for some purposes, a slave is regarded in law, as a person, yet generally he is a mere chattel personal, and *his right of personal protection belongs to his master,* who can maintain an action of trespass, for the battery of his slave. There can be, therefore, no offence against the state for a mere beating of a slave, unaccompanied by any circumstances of cruelty, or an attempt to kill and murder. The peace of the state, is not thereby broken, for a slave is not generally regarded as legally capable of being within the pale of the State,—HE IS NOT A CITIZEN, AND IS NOT IN THAT CHARACTER ENTITLED TO HER PROTECTION."

"Any person may lawfully kill a slave who has been outlawed for running away and lurking in swamps, &c,"—*Law of North Carolina.*

"A slave endevouring to entice another slave to run away, if provision be prepared for the purpose of aiding in such running away, shall be punished with *death:* and a slave who shall aid the slave so endeavoring to run away, shall also suffer *death.*"—*Law of South Carolina.*

"If a slave, when absent from his plantation, refuse to be examined by any white person, no matter what the moral character of such white person, or for what purpose he wishes to make the examination, such white person may chastise him, and if, in resisting his chastisement, he should strike the white person, by whom he is being chastised, he may be KILLED."—*Law of South Carolina.*

"If any slave shall presume to strike any white person provided such striking be not done by the command and in defence of the property of the owner, such slave shall, upon trial and conviction, before the justice or justices, suffer such punishment, for the first offence, as they shall think fit, not extending to life or limb, and for the second offence, *death.*"—*Law of Georgia.*

"If any person cut any chain or collar, which any master of slaves has put upon his slave, to prevent such slave from running away, such person will be liable to a penalty not exceeding one thousand dollars, and imprisonment not exceeding two years."—*Law of Louisiana*.

"If any person cut out the tongue, put out the eye, cruelly burn, or deprive any slave of a limb, he shall be liable to a penalty not exceeding five hundred dollars."

"If a slave be attacked by any person not having sufficient cause for so doing, and be maimed or disabled so that THE OWNER SUFFERS A LOSS FROM HIS INABILITY TO LABOUR, the person so doing, shall pay the master of such disabled slave, for the time such slave shall be off work, and for the medical attendance on the slave."—*Law of South Carolina*.

Miscellaneous

If more than seven slaves be found together in any road without a white person, they shall be liable to twenty lashes each.

If any slave visit a plantation, other than that of his master, without a written pass, he shall be liable to ten lashes.

If a slave let loose a boat from where it has been made fast, he shall for the first offence be liable to a penalty of thirty-nine lashes, and for the second, to have one ear cut from his head.—for being, on horseback, without a written permission from his master—twenty-five lashes; for riding or going abroad at night, without a written permission, a slave may be cropped or branded in the cheek, with the letter E, or otherwise punished, not extending to life, or so as to render him unfit for labour.

HENRY BOX BROWN.

FINIS

DOVER · THRIFT · EDITIONS

POETRY

101 GREAT AMERICAN POEMS, Edited by The American Poetry & Literacy Project. (0-486-40158-8)

100 BEST-LOVED POEMS, Edited by Philip Smith. (0-486-28553-7)

ENGLISH ROMANTIC POETRY: An Anthology, Edited by Stanley Appelbaum. (0-486-29282-7)

THE INFERNO, Dante Alighieri. Translated and with notes by Henry Wadsworth Longfellow. (0-486-44288-8)

PARADISE LOST, John Milton. Introduction and Notes by John A. Himes. (0-486-44287-X)

SPOON RIVER ANTHOLOGY, Edgar Lee Masters. (0-486-27275-3)

SELECTED CANTERBURY TALES, Geoffrey Chaucer. (0-486-28241-4)

SELECTED POEMS, Emily Dickinson. (0-486-26466-1)

LEAVES OF GRASS: The Original 1855 Edition, Walt Whitman. (0-486-45676-5)

COMPLETE SONNETS, William Shakespeare. (0-486-26686-9)

THE RAVEN AND OTHER FAVORITE POEMS, Edgar Allan Poe. (0-486-26685-0)

ENGLISH VICTORIAN POETRY: An Anthology, Edited by Paul Negri. (0-486-40425-0)

SELECTED POEMS, Walt Whitman. (0-486-26878-0)

THE ROAD NOT TAKEN AND OTHER POEMS, Robert Frost. (0-486-27550-7)

AFRICAN-AMERICAN POETRY: An Anthology, 1773-1927, Edited by Joan R. Sherman. (0-486-29604-0)

GREAT SHORT POEMS, Edited by Paul Negri. (0-486-41105-2)

THE RIME OF THE ANCIENT MARINER, Samuel Taylor Coleridge. (0-486-27266-4)

THE WASTE LAND, PRUFROCK AND OTHER POEMS, T. S. Eliot. (0-486-40061-1)

SONG OF MYSELF, Walt Whitman. (0-486-41410-8)

AENEID, Vergil. (0-486-28749-1)

SONGS FOR THE OPEN ROAD: Poems of Travel and Adventure, Edited by The American Poetry & Literacy Project. (0-486-40646-6)

SONGS OF INNOCENCE AND SONGS OF EXPERIENCE, William Blake. (0-486-27051-3)

WORLD WAR ONE BRITISH POETS: Brooke, Owen, Sassoon, Rosenberg and Others, Edited by Candace Ward. (0-486-29568-0)

GREAT SONNETS, Edited by Paul Negri. (0-486-28052-7)

CHRISTMAS CAROLS: Complete Verses, Edited by Shane Weller. (0-486-27397-0)

DOVER · THRIFT · EDITIONS

FICTION

FLATLAND: A ROMANCE OF MANY DIMENSIONS, Edwin A. Abbott. (0-486-27263-X)

PRIDE AND PREJUDICE, Jane Austen. (0-486-28473-5)

CIVIL WAR SHORT STORIES AND POEMS, Edited by Bob Blaisdell. (0-486-48226-X)

THE DECAMERON: Selected Tales, Giovanni Boccaccio. Edited by Bob Blaisdell. (0-486-41113-3)

JANE EYRE, Charlotte Brontë. (0-486-42449-9)

WUTHERING HEIGHTS, Emily Brontë. (0-486-29256-8)

THE THIRTY-NINE STEPS, John Buchan. (0-486-28201-5)

ALICE'S ADVENTURES IN WONDERLAND, Lewis Carroll. (0-486-27543-4)

MY ÁNTONIA, Willa Cather. (0-486-28240-6)

THE AWAKENING, Kate Chopin. (0-486-27786-0)

HEART OF DARKNESS, Joseph Conrad. (0-486-26464-5)

LORD JIM, Joseph Conrad. (0-486-40650-4)

THE RED BADGE OF COURAGE, Stephen Crane. (0-486-26465-3)

THE WORLD'S GREATEST SHORT STORIES, Edited by James Daley. (0-486-44716-2)

A CHRISTMAS CAROL, Charles Dickens. (0-486-26865-9)

GREAT EXPECTATIONS, Charles Dickens. (0-486-41586-4)

A TALE OF TWO CITIES, Charles Dickens. (0-486-40651-2)

CRIME AND PUNISHMENT, Fyodor Dostoyevsky. Translated by Constance Garnett. (0-486-41587-2)

THE ADVENTURES OF SHERLOCK HOLMES, Sir Arthur Conan Doyle. (0-486-47491-7)

THE HOUND OF THE BASKERVILLES, Sir Arthur Conan Doyle. (0-486-28214-7)

BLAKE: PROPHET AGAINST EMPIRE, David V. Erdman. (0-486-26719-9)

WHERE ANGELS FEAR TO TREAD, E. M. Forster. (0-486-27791-7)

BEOWULF, Translated by R. K. Gordon. (0-486-27264-8)

THE RETURN OF THE NATIVE, Thomas Hardy. (0-486-43165-7)

THE SCARLET LETTER, Nathaniel Hawthorne. (0-486-28048-9)

SIDDHARTHA, Hermann Hesse. (0-486-40653-9)

THE ODYSSEY, Homer. (0-486-40654-7)

THE TURN OF THE SCREW, Henry James. (0-486-26684-2)

DUBLINERS, James Joyce. (0-486-26870-5)

DOVER · THRIFT · EDITIONS

FICTION

THE METAMORPHOSIS AND OTHER STORIES, Franz Kafka. (0-486-29030-1)

SONS AND LOVERS, D. H. Lawrence. (0-486-42121-X)

THE CALL OF THE WILD, Jack London. (0-486-26472-6)

SHAKESPEARE ILLUSTRATED: Art by Arthur Rackham, Edmund Dulac, Charles Robinson and Others, Selected and Edited by Jeff A. Menges. (0-486-47890-4)

GREAT AMERICAN SHORT STORIES, Edited by Paul Negri. (0-486-42119-8)

THE GOLD-BUG AND OTHER TALES, Edgar Allan Poe. (0-486-26875-6)

ANTHEM, Ayn Rand. (0-486-49277-X)

FRANKENSTEIN, Mary Shelley. (0-486-28211-2)

THE JUNGLE, Upton Sinclair. (0-486-41923-1)

THREE LIVES, Gertrude Stein. (0-486-28059-4)

THE STRANGE CASE OF DR. JEKYLL AND MR. HYDE, Robert Louis Stevenson. (0-486-26688-5)

DRACULA, Bram Stoker. (0-486-41109-5)

UNCLE TOM'S CABIN, Harriet Beecher Stowe. (0-486-44028-1)

ADVENTURES OF HUCKLEBERRY FINN, Mark Twain. (0-486-28061-6)

THE ADVENTURES OF TOM SAWYER, Mark Twain. (0-486-40077-8)

CANDIDE, Voltaire. Edited by Francois-Marie Arouet. (0-486-26689-3)

THE COUNTRY OF THE BLIND: and Other Science-Fiction Stories, H. G. Wells. Edited by Martin Gardner. (0-486-48289-8)

THE WAR OF THE WORLDS, H. G. Wells. (0-486-29506-0)

ETHAN FROME, Edith Wharton. (0-486-26690-7)

THE PICTURE OF DORIAN GRAY, Oscar Wilde. (0-486-27807-7)

MONDAY OR TUESDAY: Eight Stories, Virginia Woolf. (0-486-29453-6)

DOVER · THRIFT · EDITIONS

NONFICTION

POETICS, Aristotle. (0-486-29577-X)

MEDITATIONS, Marcus Aurelius. (0-486-29823-X)

THE WAY OF PERFECTION, St. Teresa of Avila. Edited and Translated by E. Allison Peers. (0-486-48451-3)

THE DEVIL'S DICTIONARY, Ambrose Bierce. (0-486-27542-6)

GREAT SPEECHES OF THE 20TH CENTURY, Edited by Bob Blaisdell. (0-486-47467-4)

THE COMMUNIST MANIFESTO AND OTHER REVOLUTIONARY WRITINGS: Marx, Marat, Paine, Mao Tse-Tung, Gandhi and Others, Edited by Bob Blaisdell. (0-486-42465-0)

INFAMOUS SPEECHES: From Robespierre to Osama bin Laden, Edited by Bob Blaisdell. (0-486-47849-1)

GREAT ENGLISH ESSAYS: From Bacon to Chesterton, Edited by Bob Blaisdell. (0-486-44082-6)

GREEK AND ROMAN ORATORY, Edited by Bob Blaisdell. (0-486-49622-8)

THE UNITED STATES CONSTITUTION: The Full Text with Supplementary Materials, Edited and with supplementary materials by Bob Blaisdell. (0-486-47166-7)

GREAT SPEECHES BY NATIVE AMERICANS, Edited by Bob Blaisdell. (0-486-41122-2)

GREAT SPEECHES BY AFRICAN AMERICANS: Frederick Douglass, Sojourner Truth, Dr. Martin Luther King, Jr., Barack Obama, and Others, Edited by James Daley. (0-486-44761-8)

GREAT SPEECHES BY AMERICAN WOMEN, Edited by James Daley. (0-486-46141-6)

HISTORY'S GREATEST SPEECHES, Edited by James Daley. (0-486-49739-9)

GREAT INAUGURAL ADDRESSES, Edited by James Daley. (0-486-44577-1)

GREAT SPEECHES ON GAY RIGHTS, Edited by James Daley. (0-486-47512-3)

ON THE ORIGIN OF SPECIES: By Means of Natural Selection, Charles Darwin. (0-486-45006-6)

NARRATIVE OF THE LIFE OF FREDERICK DOUGLASS, Frederick Douglass. (0-486-28499-9)

THE SOULS OF BLACK FOLK, W. E. B. Du Bois. (0-486-28041-1)

NATURE AND OTHER ESSAYS, Ralph Waldo Emerson. (0-486-46947-6)

SELF-RELIANCE AND OTHER ESSAYS, Ralph Waldo Emerson. (0-486-27790-9)

THE LIFE OF OLAUDAH EQUIANO, Olaudah Equiano. (0-486-40661-X)

WIT AND WISDOM FROM POOR RICHARD'S ALMANACK, Benjamin Franklin. (0-486-40891-4)

THE AUTOBIOGRAPHY OF BENJAMIN FRANKLIN, Benjamin Franklin. (0-486-29073-5)

DOVER · THRIFT · EDITIONS

NONFICTION

THE DECLARATION OF INDEPENDENCE AND OTHER GREAT DOCUMENTS OF AMERICAN HISTORY: 1775-1865, Edited by John Grafton. (0-486-41124-9)

INCIDENTS IN THE LIFE OF A SLAVE GIRL, Harriet Jacobs. (0-486-41931-2)

GREAT SPEECHES, Abraham Lincoln. (0-486-26872-1)

THE WIT AND WISDOM OF ABRAHAM LINCOLN: A Book of Quotations, Abraham Lincoln. Edited by Bob Blaisdell. (0-486-44097-4)

THE SECOND TREATISE OF GOVERNMENT AND A LETTER CONCERNING TOLERATION, John Locke. (0-486-42464-2)

THE PRINCE, Niccolò Machiavelli. (0-486-27274-5)

MICHEL DE MONTAIGNE: Selected Essays, Michel de Montaigne. Translated by Charles Cotton. Edited by William Carew Hazlitt. (0-486-48603-6)

UTOPIA, Sir Thomas More. (0-486-29583-4)

BEYOND GOOD AND EVIL: Prelude to a Philosophy of the Future, Friedrich Nietzsche. (0-486-29868-X)

TWELVE YEARS A SLAVE, Solomon Northup. (0-486-78962-4)

COMMON SENSE, Thomas Paine. (0-486-29602-4)

BOOK OF AFRICAN-AMERICAN QUOTATIONS, Edited by Joslyn Pine. (0-486-47589-1)

THE TRIAL AND DEATH OF SOCRATES: Four Dialogues, Plato. (0-486-27066-1)

THE REPUBLIC, Plato. (0-486-41121-4)

SIX GREAT DIALOGUES: Apology, Crito, Phaedo, Phaedrus, Symposium, The Republic, Plato. Translated by Benjamin Jowett. (0-486-45465-7)

WOMEN'S WIT AND WISDOM: A Book of Quotations, Edited by Susan L. Rattiner. (0-486-41123-0)

GREAT SPEECHES, Franklin Delano Roosevelt. (0-486-40894-9)

THE CONFESSIONS OF ST. AUGUSTINE, St. Augustine. (0-486-42466-9)

A MODEST PROPOSAL AND OTHER SATIRICAL WORKS, Jonathan Swift. (0-486-28759-9)

THE IMITATION OF CHRIST, Thomas à Kempis. Translated by Aloysius Croft and Harold Bolton. (0-486-43185-1)

CIVIL DISOBEDIENCE AND OTHER ESSAYS, Henry David Thoreau. (0-486-27563-9)

WALDEN; OR, LIFE IN THE WOODS, Henry David Thoreau. (0-486-28495-6)

NARRATIVE OF SOJOURNER TRUTH, Sojourner Truth. (0-486-29899-X)

THE WIT AND WISDOM OF MARK TWAIN: A Book of Quotations, Mark Twain. (0-486-40664-4)

UP FROM SLAVERY, Booker T. Washington. (0-486-28738-6)

A VINDICATION OF THE RIGHTS OF WOMAN, Mary Wollstonecraft. (0-486-29036-0)

DOVER · THRIFT · EDITIONS

PLAYS

THE ORESTEIA TRILOGY: Agamemnon, the Libation-Bearers and the Furies, Aeschylus. (0-486-29242-8)

EVERYMAN, Anonymous. (0-486-28726-2)

THE BIRDS, Aristophanes. (0-486-40886-8)

LYSISTRATA, Aristophanes. (0-486-28225-2)

THE CHERRY ORCHARD, Anton Chekhov. (0-486-26682-6)

THE SEA GULL, Anton Chekhov. (0-486-40656-3)

MEDEA, Euripides. (0-486-27548-5)

FAUST, PART ONE, Johann Wolfgang von Goethe. (0-486-28046-2)

THE INSPECTOR GENERAL, Nikolai Gogol. (0-486-28500-6)

SHE STOOPS TO CONQUER, Oliver Goldsmith. (0-486-26867-5)

GHOSTS, Henrik Ibsen. (0-486-29852-3)

A DOLL'S HOUSE, Henrik Ibsen. (0-486-27062-9)

HEDDA GABLER, Henrik Ibsen. (0-486-26469-6)

DR. FAUSTUS, Christopher Marlowe. (0-486-28208-2)

TARTUFFE, Molière. (0-486-41117-6)

BEYOND THE HORIZON, Eugene O'Neill. (0-486-29085-9)

THE EMPEROR JONES, Eugene O'Neill. (0-486-29268-1)

CYRANO DE BERGERAC, Edmond Rostand. (0-486-41119-2)

MEASURE FOR MEASURE: Unabridged, William Shakespeare. (0-486-40889-2)

FOUR GREAT TRAGEDIES: Hamlet, Macbeth, Othello, and Romeo and Juliet, William Shakespeare. (0-486-44083-4)

THE COMEDY OF ERRORS, William Shakespeare. (0-486-42461-8)

HENRY V, William Shakespeare. (0-486-42887-7)

MUCH ADO ABOUT NOTHING, William Shakespeare. (0-486-28272-4)

FIVE GREAT COMEDIES: Much Ado About Nothing, Twelfth Night, A Midsummer Night's Dream, As You Like It and The Merry Wives of Windsor, William Shakespeare. (0-486-44086-9)

OTHELLO, William Shakespeare. (0-486-29097-2)

AS YOU LIKE IT, William Shakespeare. (0-486-40432-3)

ROMEO AND JULIET, William Shakespeare. (0-486-27557-4)

A MIDSUMMER NIGHT'S DREAM, William Shakespeare. (0-486-27067-X)

THE MERCHANT OF VENICE, William Shakespeare. (0-486-28492-1)

HAMLET, William Shakespeare. (0-486-27278-8)

RICHARD III, William Shakespeare. (0-486-28747-5)

DOVER · THRIFT · EDITIONS

PLAYS

THE TAMING OF THE SHREW, William Shakespeare. (0-486-29765-9)

MACBETH, William Shakespeare. (0-486-27802-6)

KING LEAR, William Shakespeare. (0-486-28058-6)

FOUR GREAT HISTORIES: Henry IV Part I, Henry IV Part II, Henry V, and Richard III, William Shakespeare. (0-486-44629-8)

THE TEMPEST, William Shakespeare. (0-486-40658-X)

JULIUS CAESAR, William Shakespeare. (0-486-26876-4)

TWELFTH NIGHT; OR, WHAT YOU WILL, William Shakespeare. (0-486-29290-8)

HEARTBREAK HOUSE, George Bernard Shaw. (0-486-29291-6)

PYGMALION, George Bernard Shaw. (0-486-28222-8)

ARMS AND THE MAN, George Bernard Shaw. (0-486-26476-9)

OEDIPUS REX, Sophocles. (0-486-26877-2)

ANTIGONE, Sophocles. (0-486-27804-2)

FIVE GREAT GREEK TRAGEDIES, Sophocles, Euripides and Aeschylus. (0-486-43620-9)

THE FATHER, August Strindberg. (0-486-43217-3)

THE PLAYBOY OF THE WESTERN WORLD AND RIDERS TO THE SEA, J. M. Synge. (0-486-27562-0)

TWELVE CLASSIC ONE-ACT PLAYS, Edited by Mary Carolyn Waldrep. (0-486-47490-9)

LADY WINDERMERE'S FAN, Oscar Wilde. (0-486-40078-6)

AN IDEAL HUSBAND, Oscar Wilde. (0-486-41423-X)

THE IMPORTANCE OF BEING EARNEST, Oscar Wilde. (0-486-26478-5)